Early praise for *Crafting Rails 4 Applications*

Superb—the most advanced Rails book on the market.

➤ **Xavier Noria**
Ruby on Rails consultant

In *Crafting Rails 4 Applications*, José Valim showed me how to make Ruby on Rails dance. I write better code and waste less time fighting the framework because of the tricks he taught me. If you make a living with Ruby on Rails (or would like to), do yourself a favor and read this book.

➤ **Avdi Grimm**
Head chef, Ruby Tapas

This is easily the best continuing-education book for Rails that I have ever read. You learn how things work internally and how you can use that to your advantage when building Rails applications.

➤ **James Edward Gray**
Developer, Gray Software Productions Inc.

Crafting Rails 4 Applications is the best introduction to Rails internals out there. After reading it I quickly became a Rails contributor.

➤ **Guillermo Iguaran**
Lead developer

Crafting Rails 4 Applications

Expert Practices for Everyday Rails Development

José Valim

The Pragmatic Bookshelf

Dallas, Texas • Raleigh, North Carolina

Many of the designations used by manufacturers and sellers to distinguish their products are claimed as trademarks. Where those designations appear in this book, and The Pragmatic Programmers, LLC was aware of a trademark claim, the designations have been printed in initial capital letters or in all capitals. The Pragmatic Starter Kit, The Pragmatic Programmer, Pragmatic Programming, Pragmatic Bookshelf, PragProg and the linking *g* device are trademarks of The Pragmatic Programmers, LLC.

Every precaution was taken in the preparation of this book. However, the publisher assumes no responsibility for errors or omissions, or for damages that may result from the use of information (including program listings) contained herein.

Our Pragmatic courses, workshops, and other products can help you and your team create better software and have more fun. For more information, as well as the latest Pragmatic titles, please visit us at *http://pragprog.com*.

The team that produced this book includes:

Brian P. Hogan (editor)
Potomac Indexing, LLC (indexer)
Candace Cunningham (copyeditor)
David J. Kelly (typesetter)
Janet Furlow (producer)
Juliet Benda (rights)
Ellie Callahan (support)

Printed in the United States of America.
ISBN-13: 978-1-937785-55-0
Printed on acid-free paper.
Book version: P1.0—November 2013

Contents

Acknowledgments

First and foremost, I am grateful to my wife for the care, for the love, and for occasionally dragging me outside to enjoy the world around us. I also want to send lots of love to my parents and family, who proudly exhibited the first edition of this book to everyone who stepped into our home. Now they will get a fresh new edition, too!

I also want to thank the guys at Plataformatec, specially George Guimarães, Hugo Baraúna, and Marcelo Park. Without them, this book would not have been possible. Everyone at Plataformatec helped from day one, when we were deciding the chapter's contents, up until the final paragraphs.

The reviewers did an outstanding job with this book. Thanks to Daniel Bretoi, Rafael França, Kevin Gisi, Jeff Holland, Landrus Kurt, Xavier Noria, Stephen Orr, Yves Senn, Neeraj Singh, and Charley Stran.

Special thanks to my editor, Brian Hogan, and The Pragmatic Programmers, who helped me take this book from great to excellent; and to Yehuda Katz for supporting me not only while writing this book, but also in Rails Core development as a whole.

Preface

When Rails was first released in 2004, it revolutionized how web development was done by embracing concepts like Don't Repeat Yourself (DRY) and convention over configuration. As Rails gained momentum, the conventions that were making things work so well started to get in the way of developers who had the urge to extend how Rails behaved or even to replace whole components.

Some developers felt that using DataMapper as an object-relational mapper (ORM) instead of using Active Record was best. Other developers turned to MongoDB and other nonrelational databases but still wanted to use their favorite web framework. Then there were developers who preferred test frameworks like RSpec to Test::Unit. These developers hacked, cobbled, or monkey-patched solutions together to accomplish their goals because previous versions of Rails did not provide a solid application programming interface (API) or the modularity required to make these changes in a clean, maintainable fashion.

With time, the Rails team started to listen to those developers, and after years the result is a robust and wide-ranging set of plug-in APIs, targeted to developers who want to customize their workflows, replace whole components, and bend Rails to their will without messy hacks.

This book guides you through these plug-in APIs with practical examples. In each chapter, we'll use test-driven development to build a Rails plug-in or application that covers those APIs and how they fit in the Rails architecture. By the time you finish this book, you will understand Rails better and increase your productivity while writing more modular and faster Rails applications.

Who Should Read This Book?

If you're an intermediate or advanced Rails developer looking to dig deeper and make the Rails framework work for you, this is your book. We'll go beyond the basics of Rails; instead of showing how Rails lets you use its built-in features to render HTML or XML from a controller, I'll show you how the render() method works so you can modify it to accept custom options, such as :pdf.

Rails Versions

All projects in *Crafting Rails 4 Applications* were developed and tested against Rails 4.0.0. Future stable releases, like Rails 4.0.1, 4.0.2, and so forth, should be suitable as well. You can check your Rails version with the following command:

```
rails -v
```

And you can use gem install to get the most appropriate version:

```
gem install rails -v 4.0.0
```

This book also has excerpts from the Rails source code. All these excerpts were extracted from Rails 4.0.0.

Most of the APIs described in this book should remain compatible throughout Rails releases. Very few of them changed since the release of the first edition of this book.[1]

Note for Windows Developers

Some chapters have dependencies that rely on C extensions. These dependencies install fine in UNIX systems, but Windows developers need the DevKit,[2] a toolkit that enables you to build many of the native C/C++ extensions available for Ruby.

Download and installation instructions are available online at http://rubyinstaller.org/downloads/. Alternatively, you can get everything you need by installing RailsInstaller,[3] which packages Ruby, Rails, and the DevKit, as well as several other common libraries.

What Is in the Book?

We'll explore the inner workings of Rails across eight chapters.

In Chapter 1, *Creating Our Own Renderer*, on page 1, I'll introduce rails plugin, a tool used throughout this book to create Rails plug-ins, and we'll customize render() to accept :pdf as an option with a behavior we'll define. This chapter starts a series of discussions about Rails's rendering stack.

---

1. http://www.pragprog.com/titles/jvrails/
2. http://rubyinstaller.org/downloads/
3. http://railsinstaller.org

In Chapter 2, *Building Models with Active Model*, on page 17, we'll take a look at Active Model and its modules as we create an extension called Mail Form that receives data through a form and sends it to a preconfigured email address.

Then in Chapter 3, *Retrieving View Templates from Custom Stores*, on page 39, we'll revisit the Rails rendering stack and customize it to read templates from a database instead of the filesystem. At the end of the chapter, you'll learn how to build faster controllers using Rails's modularity.

In Chapter 4, *Sending Multipart Emails Using Template Handlers*, on page 61, we'll create a new template handler (like ERB and Haml) on top of Markdown.[4] We'll then create new generators and seamlessly integrate them into Rails.

In Chapter 5, *Streaming Server Events to Clients Asynchronously*, on page 83, we'll build a Rails engine that streams data to clients. We'll also see how to use Ruby's Queue class in the Ruby Standard Library to synchronize the exchange of information between threads, and we'll finish with a discussion about thread safety and eager loading.

In Chapter 6, *Writing DRY Controllers with Responders*, on page 105, we'll study Rails's responders and how we can use them to encapsulate controllers' behavior, making our controllers simpler and our applications more modular. We'll then extend Rails responders to add HTTP cache and internationalized Flash messages by default. At the end of the chapter, you'll learn how to customize Rails's scaffold generators for enhanced productivity.

In Chapter 7, *Managing Application Events with Mountable Engines*, on page 131, we'll build a mountable engine that stores information about each action processed by our application in a MongoDB database and exposes them for further analysis through a web interface. We'll finish the chapter talking about Rack and its middleware stacks while writing our own middleware.

Finally, in Chapter 8, *Translating Applications Using Key-Value Back Ends*, on page 155, we'll discuss the internationalization framework (I18n) and customize it to read and store translations in a Redis data store. We'll create an application that uses Sinatra as a Rails extension so we can modify these translations from Redis through a web interface. We'll protect this translation interface using Devise and show Capybara's flexibility to write integration tests for different browsers.[5,6]

---

4. http://daringfireball.net/projects/markdown
5. https://github.com/plataformatec/devise
6. https://github.com/jnicklas/capybara

Changes in the Second Edition

All of the projects and code examples have been updated and tested to work with Rails 4. The projects also use up-to-date workflows for creating Rails plug-ins and interfacing with the framework.

In addition, Chapter 5, *Streaming Server Events to Clients Asynchronously*, on page 83, is brand-new; it covers Rails's support for Server Sent Events and digs into eager loading and thread safety.

We also explore isolated and mountable engines and single-file Rails applications in this edition.

How to Read This Book

We'll build a project from scratch in each chapter. Although these projects do not depend on each other, most of the discussions in each chapter depend on what you learned previously. For example, in Chapter 1, *Creating Our Own Renderer*, on page 1, we discuss Rails's rendering stack, and then we take this discussion further in Chapter 3, *Retrieving View Templates from Custom Stores*, on page 39, and finish it in Chapter 4, *Sending Multipart Emails Using Template Handlers*, on page 61. In other words, you can skip around, but to get the big picture, you should read the chapters in the order they are presented.

Online Resources

The book's website has links to an interactive discussion forum as well as errata for the book.[7] You'll also find the source code for all the projects we build. Readers of the ebook can click the gray box above a given code excerpt to download that snippet directly.

If you find a mistake, please create an entry on the errata page so we can address it. If you have an electronic copy of this book, please click the link in the footer of any page to easily submit errata to us.

Let's get started by creating a Rails plug-in that customizes the render() method so you can learn how Rails's rendering stack works.

José Valim
jose.valim@plataformatec.com.br

In this chapter, we'll see
- Rails plug-ins and their basic structure
- How to customize the render() method to accept custom options
- Rails rendering-stack basics

## CHAPTER 1

Creating Our Own Renderer

Like many web frameworks, Rails uses the model-view-controller (MVC) architecture pattern to organize our code. The controller usually is responsible for gathering information from our models and sending the data to the view for rendering. On other occasions, the model is responsible for representing itself, and then the view does not take part in the request; this most often happens in JavaScript Object Notation (JSON) requests. The following index action illustrates these two scenarios:

```
class PostsController < ApplicationController
  def index
    if client_authenticated?
      render json: Post.all
    else
      render template: "shared/not_authenticated", status: 401
    end
  end
end
```

The common interface to render a given model or template is the render() method. Besides knowing how to render a :template or a :file, Rails can render raw :text and a few formats, such as :xml, :json, and :js. Although the default set of Rails options is enough to bootstrap our applications, we sometimes need to add new options like :pdf or :csv to the render() method.

To achieve this, Rails provides an application programming interface (API) that we can use to create our own renderers. We'll explore this API as we modify the render() method to accept :pdf as an option and return a PDF created with Prawn,[1] a tiny, fast, and nimble PDF-writer library for Ruby.

---

1. https://github.com/prawnpdf/prawn

As in most chapters in this book, we'll use the rails plugin generator to create a plug-in that extends Rails's capabilities. Let's get started!

1.1 Creating Your First Rails Plug-in

If you already have Rails installed, you're ready to craft your first plug-in. Let's call this plug-in pdf_renderer:

```
$ rails plugin new pdf_renderer
```

When we run this command we see the following output:

```
      create
      create  README.rdoc
      create  Rakefile
      create  pdf_renderer.gemspec
      create  MIT-LICENSE
      create  .gitignore
      create  Gemfile
      create  lib/pdf_renderer.rb
      create  lib/tasks/pdf_renderer_tasks.rake
      create  lib/pdf_renderer/version.rb
      create  test/test_helper.rb
      create  test/pdf_renderer_test.rb
      append  Rakefile
   vendor_app  test/dummy
         run  bundle install
```

This command creates the basic plug-in structure, containing a pdf_renderer.gemspec file, a Rakefile, a Gemfile, and the lib and test folders. The second-to-last step in the preceding text is a little more interesting; it generates a full-fledged Rails application inside the test/dummy directory, which allows us to run our tests inside a Rails application context.

The generator finishes by running bundle install, which uses Bundler to install all dependencies our project requires.[2] With everything set up, let's explore the generated files.

pdf_renderer.gemspec

The pdf_renderer.gemspec provides a basic gem specification. The specification declares the gem's authors, version, dependencies, source files, and more. This allows us to easily bundle our plug-in into a Ruby gem, making it easy for us to share our code across different Rails applications.

Notice that the gem has the same name as the file inside the lib directory, which is pdf_renderer. By following this convention, whenever you declare this

---

2. http://gembundler.com/

gem in a Rails application's Gemfile, the file at lib/pdf_renderer.rb will be automatically required. For now, this file contains only a definition for the PdfRenderer module.

Finally, notice that our gemspec does not explicitly define the project version. Instead, the version is defined in lib/pdf_renderer/version.rb, which is referenced in the gemspec as PdfRenderer::VERSION. This is a common practice in Ruby gems.

Gemfile

In a Rails application, the Gemfile is used to list all sorts of dependencies, no matter if they're development, test, or production dependencies. However, as our plug-in already has a gemspec to list dependencies, the Gemfile simply reuses the gemspec dependencies. The Gemfile may eventually contain extra dependencies that you find convenient to use during development, like the debugger or the excellent pry gems.[3]

To manage our plug-in dependencies, we use Bundler. Bundler locks our environment to use only the gems listed in both the pdf_renderer.gemspec and the Gemfile, ensuring the tests are executed using the specified gems. We can add new dependencies and update existing ones by running the bundle install and bundle update commands in our plug-in's root.

Rakefile

The Rakefile provides basic tasks to run the test suite, generate documentation, and release our gem to the public. We can get the full list by executing rake -T at pdf_renderer's root:

```
$ rake -T
rake build          # Build pdf_renderer-0.0.1.gem into the pkg directory
rake clobber_rdoc   # Remove RDoc HTML files
rake install        # Build and install pdf_renderer-0.0.1.gem into system gems
rake rdoc           # Build RDoc HTML files
rake release        # Create tag v0.0.1 and build and push pdf_renderer...
rake rerdoc         # Rebuild RDoc HTML files
rake test           # Run tests
```

Booting the Dummy Application

rails plugin creates a dummy application inside our test directory, and this application's booting process is similar to that of a normal application created with the rails command.

---

3. http://pryrepl.org/

The config/boot.rb file has only one responsibility: to configure our application's load paths. The config/application.rb file should then load all required dependencies and configure the application, which is initialized in config/environment.rb.

The boot file that rails plugin generates is at test/dummy/config/boot.rb, and it is similar to the application one—the first difference is that it needs to point to the Gemfile at the root of the pdf_renderer plugin. It also explicitly adds the plug-in's lib directory to Ruby's load path, making our plug-in available inside the dummy application:

```
pdf_renderer/1_prawn/test/dummy/config/boot.rb
# Set up gems listed in the Gemfile.
ENV['BUNDLE_GEMFILE'] ||= File.expand_path('../../../../Gemfile', __FILE__)

require 'bundler/setup' if File.exists?(ENV['BUNDLE_GEMFILE'])
$LOAD_PATH.unshift File.expand_path('../../../../lib', __FILE__)
```

The boot file delegates to Bundler the responsibility of setting up dependencies and their load paths. The test/dummy/config/application.rb is a stripped-down version of the config/application.rb found in Rails applications:

```
pdf_renderer/1_prawn/test/dummy/config/application.rb
require File.expand_path('../boot', __FILE__)
require 'rails/all'

Bundler.require(*Rails.groups)
require "pdf_renderer"

module Dummy
  class Application < Rails::Application
    # ...
  end
end
```

The config/environment.rb is exactly the same as you'd find in a regular Rails application:

```
pdf_renderer/1_prawn/test/dummy/config/environment.rb
# Load the rails application.
require File.expand_path('../application', __FILE__)

# Initialize the rails application.
Dummy::Application.initialize!
```

Running Tests

By default rails plugin generates one sanity test for our plug-in. Let's run our tests and see them pass with the following:

```
$ rake test
```

The output looks something like this:

```
Run options: --seed 20094

# Running tests:

.

Finished tests in 0.096440s, 10.3691 tests/s, 10.3691 assertions/s.

1 tests, 1 assertions, 0 failures, 0 errors, 0 skips
```

The test, defined in test/pdf_renderer_test.rb, asserts that our plug-in defined a module called PdfRenderer.

```
pdf_renderer/1_prawn/test/pdf_renderer_test.rb
require 'test_helper'
class PdfRendererTest < ActiveSupport::TestCase
  test "truth" do
    assert_kind_of Module, PdfRenderer
  end
end
```

Finally, note that our test file requires test/test_helper.rb, which is the file responsible for loading our application and configuring our testing environment. With our plug-in skeleton created and a green test suite, we can start writing our first custom renderer.

1.2 Writing the Renderer

At the beginning of this chapter, we briefly discussed the render() method and a few options that it accepts, but we haven't formally described what a *renderer* is.

A renderer is nothing more than a hook exposed by the render() method to customize its behavior. Adding our own renderer to Rails is quite simple. Let's consider the :json renderer in Rails source code as an example:

```
rails/actionpack/lib/action_controller/metal/renderers.rb
add :json do |json, options|
  json = json.to_json(options) unless json.kind_of?(String)
  if options[:callback].present?
    self.content_type ||= Mime::JS
    "#{options[:callback]}(#{json})"
  else
    self.content_type ||= Mime::JSON
    json
  end
end
```

So, whenever we invoke the following method in our application

```
render json: @post
```

it will invoke the block defined as the :json renderer. The local variable json inside the block points to the @post object, and the other options passed to render() will be available in the options variable. In this case, since the method was called without any extra options, it's an empty hash.

In the following sections, we want to add a :pdf renderer that creates a PDF document from a given template and sends it to the client with the appropriate headers. The value given to the :pdf option should be the name of the file to be sent.

The following is an example of the API we want to provide:

```
render pdf: 'contents', template: 'path/to/template'
```

Although Rails knows how to render templates and send files to the client, it does not know how to handle PDF files. For this, let's use Prawn.

Playing with Prawn

Prawn is a PDF-writing library for Ruby.[4] Since it's going to be a dependency of our plug-in, we need to add it to our pdf_renderer.gemspec:

```
pdf_renderer/1_prawn/pdf_renderer.gemspec
s.add_dependency "prawn", "0.12.0"
```

Next, let's ask bundler to install our new dependency and test it via interactive Ruby:

```
$ bundle install
$ irb
```

Inside irb, let's create a sample PDF:

```
require "prawn"

pdf = Prawn::Document.new
pdf.text("A PDF in four lines of code")
pdf.render_file("sample.pdf")
```

Exit irb, and you can see a PDF file in the directory in which you started the irb session. Prawn provides its own syntax to create PDFs, and although this gives us a flexible API, the drawback is that it cannot create PDFs from HTML files.

---

4.   https://github.com/prawnpdf/prawn

Code in Action

Let's write some tests before we dive into the code. Since we have a dummy application at test/dummy, we can create controllers as in an actual Rails application, and use them to test the complete request stack. Let's name the controller used in our tests HomeController and add the following contents:

```
pdf_renderer/1_prawn/test/dummy/app/controllers/home_controller.rb
class HomeController < ApplicationController
  def index
    respond_to do |format|
      format.html
      format.pdf { render pdf: "contents" }
    end
  end
end
```

Now let's create the PDF view the controller uses:

```
pdf_renderer/1_prawn/test/dummy/app/views/home/index.pdf.erb
This template is rendered with Prawn.
```

And add a route for the index action:

```
pdf_renderer/1_prawn/test/dummy/config/routes.rb
Dummy::Application.routes.draw do
  get "/home", to: "home#index", as: :home
end
```

Finally, let's write an integration test that verifies a PDF is being returned when we access /home.pdf:

```
pdf_renderer/1_prawn/test/integration/pdf_delivery_test.rb
require "test_helper"

class PdfDeliveryTest < ActionDispatch::IntegrationTest
  test "pdf request sends a pdf as file" do
    get home_path(format: :pdf)

    assert_match "PDF", response.body
    assert_equal "binary", headers["Content-Transfer-Encoding"]

    assert_equal "attachment; filename=\"contents.pdf\"",
      headers["Content-Disposition"]
    assert_equal "application/pdf", headers["Content-Type"]
  end
end
```

The test uses the response headers to assert that a binary-encoded PDF file was sent as an attachment, including the expected filename. Although we cannot assert much about the PDF body since it's encoded, we can at least assert that it has the string PDF in it, which Prawn adds to the PDF body. Let's run our test with rake test and watch it fail:

```
1) Failure:
test_pdf_request_sends_a_pdf_as_file(PdfDeliveryTest):
Expected /PDF/ to match "This template is rendered with Prawn.\n".
```

The test fails as expected. Since we haven't taught Rails how to handle the :pdf option in render(), it is simply rendering the template without wrapping it in a PDF. We can make the test pass by implementing our renderer in just a few lines of code inside lib/pdf_renderer.rb:

```
pdf_renderer/1_prawn/lib/pdf_renderer.rb
require "prawn"
ActionController::Renderers.add :pdf do |filename, options|
  pdf = Prawn::Document.new
  pdf.text render_to_string(options)
  send_data(pdf.render, filename: "#{filename}.pdf",
    disposition: "attachment")
end
```

And that's it! In this code block, we create a new PDF document, add some text to it, and send the PDF as an attachment using the send_data() method available in Rails. We can now run the tests and watch them pass. We can also go to test/dummy, start the server with rails server, and test it by accessing *http://localhost:3000/home.pdf.*

Even though our test passes, there is still some explaining to do. First of all, observe that we did not, at any point, set the Content-Type to application/pdf. How did Rails know which content type to set in our response?

The content type was set correctly because Rails ships with a set of registered formats and MIME types:

```
rails/actionpack/lib/action_dispatch/http/mime_types.rb
Mime::Type.register "text/html", :html, %w( application/xhtml+xml ), %w( xhtml )
Mime::Type.register "text/plain", :text, [], %w(txt)
Mime::Type.register "text/javascript", :js,
  %w(application/javascript application/x-javascript)
Mime::Type.register "text/css", :css
Mime::Type.register "text/calendar", :ics
Mime::Type.register "text/csv", :csv

Mime::Type.register "image/png", :png, [], %w(png)
Mime::Type.register "image/jpeg", :jpeg, [], %w(jpg jpeg jpe pjpeg)
Mime::Type.register "image/gif", :gif, [], %w(gif)
Mime::Type.register "image/bmp", :bmp, [], %w(bmp)
Mime::Type.register "image/tiff", :tiff, [], %w(tif tiff)
```

```
Mime::Type.register "video/mpeg", :mpeg, [], %w(mpg mpeg mpe)

Mime::Type.register "application/xml", :xml, %w(text/xml application/x-xml)
Mime::Type.register "application/rss+xml", :rss
Mime::Type.register "application/atom+xml", :atom
Mime::Type.register "application/x-yaml", :yaml, %w( text/yaml )

Mime::Type.register "multipart/form-data", :multipart_form
Mime::Type.register "application/x-www-form-urlencoded", :url_encoded_form

Mime::Type.register "application/json", :json,
  %w(text/x-json application/jsonrequest)

Mime::Type.register "application/pdf", :pdf, [], %w(pdf)
Mime::Type.register "application/zip", :zip, [], %w(zip)
```

Notice how the PDF format is defined with its respective content type. When we requested the /home.pdf URL, Rails retrieved the pdf format from the URL, verified it matched with the format.pdf block defined in HomeController#index, and proceeded to set the proper content type before invoking the block that called render.

Going back to our render implementation, although send_data() is a public Rails method and has been available since the first Rails versions, you might not have heard about the render_to_string() method. To better understand it, let's take a look at the Rails rendering process as a whole.

1.3   Understanding the Rails Rendering Stack

Action Mailer and Action Controller have several features in common, such as template rendering, helpers, and layouts. To avoid code duplication, those shared responsibilities are centralized in Abstract Controller, which both Action Mailer and Action Controller use as their foundation. At the same time, some features are required by only one of the two libraries. Given those requirements, Abstract Controller was designed in a way that developers can cherry-pick the functionality they want. For instance, if we want an object to have basic rendering capabilities, where it simply renders a template but does not include a layout, we include the AbstractController::Rendering module in our object, leaving out AbstractController::Layouts.

When we include AbstractController::Rendering in an object, the rendering stack proceeds as shown in Figure 1, *Visualization of the rendering stack when we call render with AbstractController::Rendering*, on page 10 every time we call render().

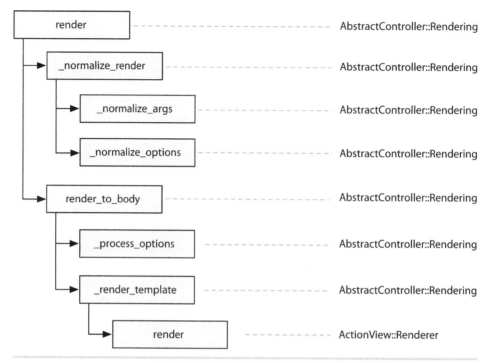

Figure 1—Visualization of the rendering stack when we call render() with AbstractController::Rendering

Each rectangle represents a method, followed by the classes or modules that implement it. The arrows represent method calls. For example, render() calls _normalize_render() and then calls render_to_body(). The stack can be confirmed by looking at the AbstractController::Rendering implementation in Rails source code:

```
rails/actionpack/lib/abstract_controller/rendering.rb
def render(*args, &block)
  options = _normalize_render(*args, &block)
  self.response_body = render_to_body(options)
end

def _normalize_render(*args, &block)
  options = _normalize_args(*args, &block)
  _normalize_options(options)
  options
end

def render_to_body(options = {})
  _process_options(options)
  _render_template(options)
end
```

Abstract Controller's rendering stack is responsible for normalizing the arguments and options you provide and converting them to a hash of options that ActionView::Renderer#render() accepts, which will take care of finally rendering the template. Each method in the stack plays a specific role within this overall responsibility. These methods can be either private (starting with an underscore) or part of the public API.

The first relevant method in the stack is _normalize_args(), invoked by _normalized_render(), and it converts the user-provided arguments into a hash. This allows the render() method to be invoked as render(:new), which _normalize_args() converts to render(action: "new"). The hash that _normalize_args() returns is then further normalized by _normalize_options(). There is not much normalization happening inside AbstractController::Rendering#_normalize_options() since it's the basic module, but it does convert render(partial: true) calls to render(partial: action_name). So, whenever you give partial: true in a show() action, it becomes partial: "show" down the stack.

After normalization, render_to_body() is invoked. This is where the actual rendering starts. The first step is to process all options that are meaningless to the view, using the _process_options() method. Although AbstractController::Rendering#_process_options() is an empty method, we can look into ActionController::Rendering#_process_options() for a handful of examples about what to do in this method. For instance, in controllers we are allowed to invoke the following:

```
render template: "shared/not_authenticated", status: 401
```

Here the :status option is meaningless to views, since status refers to the HTTP response status. So, it's ActionController::Rendering#_process_options()'s responsibility to intercept and handle this option and others.

After options processing, _render_template() is invoked and different objects start to collaborate. In particular, an instance of ActionView::Renderer called view_renderer is created and the render() method is called on it with two arguments: the view_context and our hash of normalized options:

rails/actionpack/lib/abstract_controller/rendering.rb
```
view_renderer.render(view_context, options)
```

The *view context* is an instance of ActionView::Base; it is the context in which our templates are evaluated. When we call link_to() in a template, it works because it's a method available inside ActionView::Base. When instantiated, the view context receives view_assigns() as an argument. The term *assigns* references the group of controller variables that will be accessible in the view. By default, whenever you set an instance variable in your controller as @posts = Post.all, @posts is marked as an *assign* and will also be available in views.

At this point, it's important to highlight the inversion of concerns that happened between Rails 2.3 and Rails 3.0. In the former the view is responsible for retrieving assigns from the controller, and in the latter the controller *tells* the view which assigns to use.

Imagine that we want a controller that does not send any assigns to the view. In Rails 2.3, since the view automatically pulls in all instance variables from controllers, to achieve that we should either stop using instance variables in our controller or be sure to remove all instance variables before rendering a template. In Rails 3 and up, this responsibility is handled in the controller. We just need to override the view_assigns() method to return an empty hash:

```
class UsersController < ApplicationController
  protected
  def view_assigns
    {}
  end
end
```

By returning an empty hash, we ensure none of the actions in the controller pass assigns to the view.

With the view context and the hash of normalized options in hand, our ActionView::Renderer instance has everything it needs to find a template, based on the options, and finally render it inside the view context.

This modular and well-defined stack allows anyone to hook into the rendering process and add their own features. When we include AbstractController::Layouts on top of AbstractController::Rendering, the rendering stack is extended as shown in Figure 2, *Visualization of the rendering stack when we call render with AbstractController::Rendering and AbstractController::Layouts*, on page 13.

AbstractController::Layouts simply overrides _normalize_options() to support the :layout option. In case no :layout option is set when calling render(), one may be automatically set based on the value a developer configures at the controller class level. Action Controller further extends the Abstract Controller rendering stack, adding and processing options that make sense only in the controller scope. Those extensions are broken into four main modules:

- ActionController::Rendering: Overrides render() to check if it's ever called twice, raising a DoubleRenderError if so; also overrides _process_options() to handle options such as :location, :status, and :content_type

- ActionController::Renderers: Adds the API we used in this chapter, which allows us to trigger a specific behavior whenever a given key (such as :pdf) is supplied

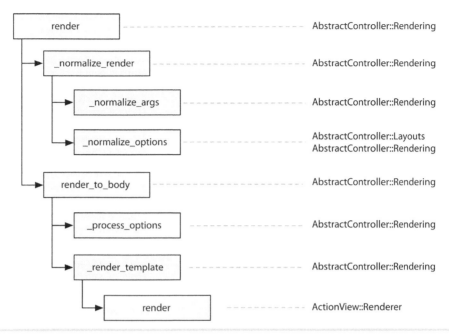

Figure 2—Visualization of the rendering stack when we call render() with AbstractController::Rendering and AbstractController::Layouts

- ActionController::Instrumentation: Overloads the render() method so it can measure how much time was spent in the rendering stack

- ActionController::Streaming: Overloads the _process_options() method to handle the :stream by setting the proper HTTP headers and the _render_template() method to allow templates to be streamed

Figure 3, *Visualization of the rendering stack when we call render with AbstractController and ActionController*, on page 14 shows the final stack with Abstract Controller and Action Controller rendering modules.

Now that we understand how the render() works, we are ready to understand how render_to_string() works. Let's start by seeing its definition in AbstractController::Rendering:

```
rails/actionpack/lib/abstract_controller/rendering.rb
def render_to_string(*args, &block)
  options = _normalize_render(*args, &block)
  render_to_body(options)
end
```

At first, the render_to_string() method looks quite similar to render(). The only difference is that render_to_string() does not store the rendered template as the

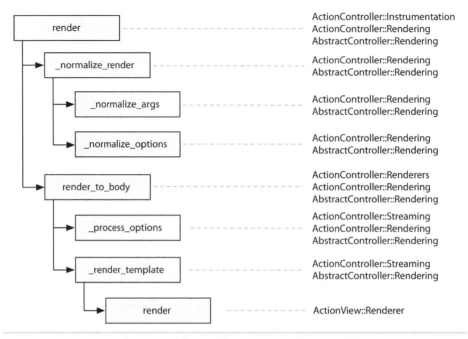

Figure 3—Visualization of the rendering stack when we call render() with AbstractController and ActionController

response body. However, when we analyze the whole rendering stack, we see that some Action Controller modules overload render() to add behavior while leaving render_to_string() alone.

For instance, by using render_to_string() in our renderer, we ensure instrumentation events defined by ActionController::Instrumentation won't be triggered twice and won't raise a double render error since those functionalities are added only to the render() method.

In some other cases, render_to_string() may be overloaded, as well. When using Action Controller, the response body can be another object that is not a string, which is what happens on template streaming. For this reason, ActionController::Rendering overrides render_to_string() to always return a string, as the name indicates.

1.4 Taking It to the Next Level

Going back to our renderer implementation, we now understand what happens when we add the following line to our controllers:

```
format.pdf { render pdf: "contents" }
```

In our renderer, it becomes this:

```
pdf = Prawn::Document.new
pdf.text render_to_string({})
send_data(pdf.render, filename: "contents.pdf",
  disposition: "attachment")
```

When we invoke render_to_string() with an empty hash, the _normalize_options()
method in the rendering stack detects the empty hash and changes it to
render the template with the same name as the current action. At the end,
render_to_string({}) simply passes template: "#{controller_name}/#{action_name}" to the
view-renderer object.

The fact that our renderer relies on render_to_string() allows us to also use the
following options:

```
render pdf: "contents", template: "path/to/template"
```

And internally, the preceding code is the same as the following:

```
pdf = Prawn::Document.new
pdf.text render_to_string(template: "path/to/template")
send_data(pdf.render, filename: "contents.pdf",
  disposition: "attachment")
```

This time render_to_string() receives an explicit template to render. To finish our
PDF renderer, let's add a test to confirm that the chosen template will indeed
be rendered. Our test invokes a new action in HomeController that calls render()
with both :pdf and :template options:

pdf_renderer/2_final/test/dummy/app/controllers/home_controller.rb
```
def another
  render pdf: "contents", template: "home/index"
end
```

Let's add a route for this new action:

pdf_renderer/2_final/test/dummy/config/routes.rb
```
get "/another", to: "home#another", as: :another
```

Our test simply accesses "/another.pdf" and ensures a PDF is being returned:

pdf_renderer/2_final/test/integration/pdf_delivery_test.rb
```
test "pdf renderer uses the specified template" do
  get another_path(format: :pdf)
  assert_match "PDF", response.body
  assert_equal "binary", headers["Content-Transfer-Encoding"]
  assert_equal "attachment; filename=\"contents.pdf\"",
    headers["Content-Disposition"]
  assert_equal "application/pdf", headers["Content-Type"]
end
```

Now run the tests and watch them pass once again!

1.5   Wrapping Up

In this chapter we created a renderer for the PDF format. Using these ideas, you can easily create renderers for formats such as CSV and ATOM and encapsulate any logic specific to your application in a renderer, as well. You could even create a wrapper for other PDF libraries that are able to convert HTML files to PDF, such as the paid Prince XML library or the open source Flying Saucer, which is written in Java but is easily accessible through JRuby.[5,6,7]

We also discussed the Rails rendering stack and its modularity. As Rails itself relies on this well-defined stack to extend Action Controller and Action Mailer, it makes the rendering API more robust; it was battle-tested by Rails's own features and various use cases. As we'll see in the chapters that follow, this is a common practice throughout the Rails codebase.

Rails's renderers open several possibilities to extend your rendering stack. But as with any other powerful tool, remember to use renderers wisely.

Next let's look at Active Model and its modules and create a Rails extension to use in Rails controllers and views.

5.   http://www.princexml.com/

6.   http://xhtmlrenderer.java.net/

7.   http://jruby.org/

In this chapter, we'll see
  • Active Model and its modules
  • How to make an object comply with the Active Model API
    required by Rails
  • Rails's validators and Ruby-constant lookup

CHAPTER 2

Building Models with Active Model

In the previous chapter, we talked briefly about Abstract Controller and how it reduced code duplication in the Rails source code since it's decoupled from both Action Mailer and Action Controller. Now let's look at Active Model, which is similar.

Active Model was originally created to hold the behavior shared between Active Record and Active Resource.[1] As with Abstract Controller, the desired functionalities can be cherry-picked by including only the modules you need. Active Model is also responsible for defining the application programming interface (API) required by Rails controllers and views, so any other object-relational mapper (ORM) can use Active Model to ensure Rails behaves exactly as it would with Active Record.

Let's explore both facets of Active Model in this chapter by writing a plug-in called *Mail Form* that we'll use in our controllers and views. Mail Form's goal is to receive a hash of parameters sent by a POST request, validate them, and email them to a specified email address. This abstraction will allow us to create fully functional contact forms in just a couple of minutes!

2.1 Creating Our Model

Mail Form objects belong to the models part in the model-view-controller architecture, as they receive the information sent through a form and deliver it to a recipient specified by the business model. Let's structure Mail Form in the same way Active Record works: we'll provide a class named MailForm::Base that contains the most common features we expect in a model, such as the ability to specify attributes, and seamless integration with Rails forms. As we did in the previous chapter, let's use rails plugin to create our new plug-in:

---

1. Since then, Active Resource has been extracted from the Rails codebase and is available at https://github.com/rails/activeresource.

```
$ rails plugin new mail_form
```

Our first feature is to implement a class method called attributes() that allows a developer to specify which attributes the Mail Form object contains. Let's create a model inside test/fixtures/sample_mail.rb as a fixture to use in our tests:

mail_form/1_attributes/test/fixtures/sample_mail.rb
```
class SampleMail < MailForm::Base
  attributes :name, :email
end
```

Then we'll add a test to ensure the defined attributes name and email are available as accessors in the Mail Form object:

mail_form/1_attributes/test/mail_form_test.rb
```
require "test_helper"
require "fixtures/sample_mail"

class MailFormTest < ActiveSupport::TestCase
  test "sample mail has name and email as attributes" do
    sample = SampleMail.new
    sample.name = "User"
    assert_equal "User", sample.name
    sample.email = "user@example.com"
    assert_equal "user@example.com", sample.email
  end
end
```

When we run the test suite with rake test, it fails because MailForm::Base is not defined yet. Let's define it in lib/mail_form/base.rb and implement the attributes() method:

mail_form/1_attributes/lib/mail_form/base.rb
```
module MailForm
  class Base
    def self.attributes(*names)
      attr_accessor(*names)
    end
  end
end
```

Our implementation delegates the creation of attributes to attr_accessor(). Before we run our tests again, we need to ensure that MailForm::Base is loaded. One option would be to explicitly require "mail_form/base" in lib/mail_form.rb. However, let's use Ruby's autoload() instead:

mail_form/1_attributes/lib/mail_form.rb
```
module MailForm
  autoload :Base, "mail_form/base"
end
```

autoload() allows us to lazily load a constant when it is first referenced. So we note that MailForm has a constant called Base defined in mail_form/base.rb. When MailForm::Base is referenced for the first time, Ruby loads the mail_form/base.rb file. This is frequently used in Ruby gems and in Rails itself for a fast booting process, as it does not need to load everything up front.

With autoload() in place, our first test passes. We have a simple model with attributes, but so far we haven't used any of Active Model's goodness. Let's do that now.

Adding Attribute Methods

ActiveModel::AttributeMethods is a module that tracks all defined attributes, allowing us to add a common behavior to all of them dynamically. To show how it works, let's define two convenience methods, clear_name() and clear_email(), which will clear out the value of the associated attribute when invoked. Let's write a test first:

```
mail_form/2_attributes_prefix/test/mail_form_test.rb
test "sample mail can clear attributes using clear_ prefix" do
  sample = SampleMail.new

  sample.name  = "User"
  sample.email = "user@example.com"
  assert_equal "User", sample.name
  assert_equal "user@example.com", sample.email

  sample.clear_name
  sample.clear_email
  assert_nil sample.name
  assert_nil sample.email
end
```

Invoking clear_name() and clear_email() sets their respective attribute value back to nil. With ActiveModel::AttributeMethods, we can define both clear_name() and clear_email() dynamically in four simple steps, as outlined in our new MailForm::Base implementation:

```
mail_form/2_attributes_prefix/lib/mail_form/base.rb
module MailForm

  class Base
    include ActiveModel::AttributeMethods  # 1) attribute methods behavior
    attribute_method_prefix 'clear_'       # 2) clear_ is attribute prefix

    def self.attributes(*names)
      attr_accessor(*names)
```

```ruby
    # 3) Ask to define the prefix methods for the given attribute names
    define_attribute_methods(names)
  end

  protected

  # 4) Since we declared a "clear_" prefix, it expects to have a
  # "clear_attribute" method defined, which receives an attribute
  # name and implements the clearing logic.
  def clear_attribute(attribute)
    send("#{attribute}=", nil)
  end
  end
end
```

Run rake test, and all tests should be green again. ActiveModel::AttributeMethods uses method_missing() to compile both the clear_name() and clear_email() methods when they are first accessed. Their implementation invokes clear_attribute(), passing the attribute name as a parameter.

If we want to define suffixes instead of a prefix like clear_, we need to use the attribute_method_suffix() method and implement the method with the chosen suffix logic. As an example, let's implement name?() and email?() methods, which should return true if the respective attribute value is present, as in the following test:

mail_form/3_attributes_suffix/test/mail_form_test.rb
```ruby
test "sample mail can ask if an attribute is present or not" do
  sample = SampleMail.new
  assert !sample.name?

  sample.name = "User"
  assert sample.name?

  sample.email = ""
  assert !sample.email?
end
```

When we run the test suite, our new test fails. To make it pass, let's define ? as a suffix, changing our MailForm::Base implementation to the following:

mail_form/3_attributes_suffix/lib/mail_form/base.rb
```ruby
module MailForm

  class Base
    include ActiveModel::AttributeMethods
    attribute_method_prefix 'clear_'

    # 1) Add the attribute suffix
    attribute_method_suffix '?'
```

```ruby
    def self.attributes(*names)
      attr_accessor(*names)
      define_attribute_methods(names)
    end
    protected

    def clear_attribute(attribute)
      send("#{attribute}=", nil)
    end
    # 2) Implement the logic required by the '?' suffix
    def attribute?(attribute)
      send(attribute).present?
    end
  end
end
```

Now we have both prefix and suffix methods defined and the tests are passing. But what if we want to define both the prefix and the suffix at the same time? We could use the attribute_method_affix() method, which accepts a hash specifying both the prefix and the suffix.

Active Record uses attribute methods extensively. An example is the attribute_before_type_cast() method, which uses _before_type_cast as a suffix to return raw data, as received from forms. The dirty functionality, which is also part of Active Model, is built on top of ActiveModel::AttributeMethods and defines a handful of methods like attribute_changed?(), reset_attribute!(), and so on. You can check the dirty implementation source code in the Rails repository.[2]

Aiming for an Active Model–Compliant API

Even though we added attributes to our models to store form data, we need to ensure that our model complies with the Active Model API; otherwise, we won't be able to use it in our controllers and views.

As usual, we'll achieve this compliance through test-driven development, except this time we won't need to write the tests—Rails already provides all of them in a module called ActiveModel::Lint::Tests. When included, this module defines several tests asserting that each method required in an Active Model–compliant API exists. Each of these tests expects an instance variable named @model to return the object we want to assert against. In our case, @model should contain an instance of SampleMail, which will be compliant if MailForm::Base is compliant. Let's create a new test file called test/compliance_test.rb with the following:

---

2.   https://github.com/rails/rails/tree/4-0-stable/activemodel/lib/active_model/dirty.rb

```
mail_form/4_am_compliance/test/compliance_test.rb
require 'test_helper'
require 'fixtures/sample_mail'

class ComplianceTest < ActiveSupport::TestCase
  include ActiveModel::Lint::Tests

  def setup
    @model = SampleMail.new
  end
end
```

When we run rake test, we get several failures, all with this reason:

```
The object should respond to to_model.
```

When Rails controllers and view helpers receive a model, they first call to_model() and manipulate the returned result instead of the model directly. This allows ORM implementations that don't want to add Active Model methods to their API to return a proxy object where these methods are defined. In our case, we want to add Active Model methods directly to MailForm::Base. Consequently, our to_model() implementation should return self, as shown here:

```
def to_model
  self
end
```

Although we could add this method to MailForm::Base, we are not going to implement it ourselves. Instead, let's include ActiveModel::Conversion, which implements to_model() exactly as we discussed, and three other methods required by Active Model: to_key(), to_param(), and to_partial_path().

The to_key() method should return an array of keys that uniquely identifies the model, if any exists, and it is used by dom_id() in views. The dom_id() method was added to Rails along with dom_class() and a bunch of other helpers to better organize our views. For example, div_for(@post), where @post is an Active Record instance of the Post class with an id of 42, relies on both these methods to create a div where the id attribute is equal to post_42 and the class attribute is post. For Active Record, to_key() returns an array containing the record ID from the database.

On the other hand, to_param() is used in routing and can be overwritten in any model to generate a unique URL for that model. When we invoke post_path(@post), Rails calls to_param() in the @post object and uses its result to generate the final URL. For Active Record, the default is to return the ID as a string.

Finally, we have to_partial_path(). This method is invoked every time we pass a record or a collection of records to render() in our views. Rails will go through each of these records and retrieve the path to their partial. For example, the path to an instance of the Post class is posts/post.

It is important to understand not only what those methods do, but also what they allow us to achieve. For example, by customizing to_param(), we can easily change the URLs of our objects. Imagine a Post class with id and title attributes; changing the URLs of those posts to include the title is as easy as this:

```
def to_param
  "#{id}-#{title.parameterize}"
end
```

Similarly, imagine that each Post has a different format. It can be a video, a link, or a bunch of a text, and each of those formats should be rendered differently. If we store the format of the blog post in the format attribute, we could render each post as follows:

```
@posts.each do |post|
  render partial: "posts/post_#{post.format}",
    locals: { post: @post }
end
```

However, by overriding to_partial_path() like this

```
def to_partial_path
  "posts/post_#{format}"
end
```

our view would simply call

```
render @posts
```

This not only makes our code cleaner, but also improves our application performance. In the first example, we end up going through Rails's rendering stack many times, looking up templates and duplicating efforts. However, by customizing to_partial_path(), we call render() just once, allowing Rails to efficiently look up all partials in one take.

The default to_partial_path() implementation available in ActiveModel::Conversion allows us to provide partials for MailForm::Base objects as in any Active Record object. However, since our objects are never persisted, they aren't uniquely identified, meaning that both to_key() and to_param() should return nil. This is exactly the behavior provided by ActiveModel::Conversion. Let's include it in our MailForm::Base class:

```
mail_form/4_am_compliance/lib/mail_form/base.rb
module MailForm
  class Base
    include ActiveModel::Conversion
```

When we include this module and run rake test, we get errors with the following messages (you may get them in different order):

```
The model should respond to model_name
```

```
The model should respond to errors
```

```
The model should respond to persisted?
```

To fix the first failing test, we need to extend the MailForm::Base class with ActiveModel::Naming:

```
mail_form/4_am_compliance/lib/mail_form/base.rb
module MailForm
  class Base
    include ActiveModel::Conversion
    extend ActiveModel::Naming
```

After we extend our class with ActiveModel::Naming, it responds to a method called model_name() that returns an instance of ActiveModel::Name, which acts like a string and provides a few methods, such as human(), singular(), and others that are inflected from the model name. Let's add a small test case to our suite to show these methods and what they return:

```
mail_form/4_am_compliance/test/compliance_test.rb
test "model_name exposes singular and human name" do
  assert_equal "sample_mail", @model.class.model_name.singular
  assert_equal "Sample mail", @model.class.model_name.human
end
```

This is similar to the behavior Active Record exhibits. The only difference is that Active Record supports internationalization (I18n) and Mail Form does not. Luckily, that can be easily fixed by extending MailForm::Base with ActiveModel::Translation. Let's write a test first:

```
mail_form/4_am_compliance/test/compliance_test.rb
test "model_name.human uses I18n" do
  begin
    I18n.backend.store_translations :en,
      activemodel: { models: { sample_mail: "My Sample Mail" } }

    assert_equal "My Sample Mail", @model.class.model_name.human
  ensure
    I18n.reload!
  end
end
```

The test adds a new translation to the I18n back end that contains the desired human name for the SampleMail class. We need to wrap the code in the begin...ensure clause to guarantee the I18n back end is reloaded, removing the translation we stored. Let's update MailForm::Base to make the new test pass:

mail_form/4_am_compliance/lib/mail_form/base.rb
```ruby
module MailForm
  class Base
    include ActiveModel::Conversion
    extend ActiveModel::Naming
    extend ActiveModel::Translation
```

After we add naming and translation behaviors, rake test returns fewer failures, showing that we're moving forward. This time our tests fail for the following reasons:

```
The model should respond to errors
```

```
The model should respond to persisted?
```

The first failure is related to validations. Active Model does not say anything about validation macros (such as validates_presence_of()), but it requires us to define a method named errors(), which returns a Hash, and each value in this hash is an Array. We can fix this failure by including ActiveModel::Validations in our model:

mail_form/4_am_compliance/lib/mail_form/base.rb
```ruby
module MailForm
  class Base
    include ActiveModel::Conversion
    extend ActiveModel::Naming
    extend ActiveModel::Translation
    include ActiveModel::Validations
```

Now our model instance responds to errors() and valid?(), which behaves exactly as in Active Record. Furthermore, ActiveModel::Validations adds several validation macros, such as validates(), validates_format_of(), and validates_inclusion_of().

For now, let's run rake test and see what's left to make our test suite green again:

```
The model should respond to persisted?
```

This time Rails won't help us. Luckily, it's easy enough to implement persisted?() ourselves. Both our controllers and our views use the persisted?() method, under different circumstances. For instance, whenever we invoke form_for(@model), it checks whether the model is persisted. If so, it creates a form that does a PUT request; if not, it should do a POST request. The same happens in url_for() when it generates a URL based on your model.

In Active Record, the object is persisted if it's saved in the database; in other words, if it's neither a new record nor destroyed. However, in our case, our object won't be saved in any database, and consequently persisted?() should always return false.

Let's add the persisted?() method to our MailForm::Base implementation:

```
mail_form/4_am_compliance/lib/mail_form/base.rb
def persisted?
  false
end
```

This time, after running rake test, all tests pass! This means our model complies with the Active Model API. Well done!

Delivering the Form

The next step in our Mail Form implementation is to add the logic that delivers an email with the model attributes. The deliver() method takes care of the delivery, and sends an email to the address stored in our model's email attribute. The email body contains all model attributes and their respective values. Let's specify this behavior by adding a new test to test/mail_form_test.rb:

```
mail_form/5_delivery/test/mail_form_test.rb
setup do
  ActionMailer::Base.deliveries.clear
end

test "delivers an email with attributes" do
  sample = SampleMail.new
  # Simulate data from the form
  sample.email = "user@example.com"
  sample.deliver

  assert_equal 1, ActionMailer::Base.deliveries.size
  mail = ActionMailer::Base.deliveries.last

  assert_equal ["user@example.com"], mail.from
  assert_match "Email: user@example.com", mail.body.encoded
end
```

When we run the new test, we get a failure because the deliver() method does not exist yet. Because our model has the concept of validity from ActiveModel::Validations, the deliver() method should deliver the email if the Mail Form object is valid?():

mail_form/5_delivery/lib/mail_form/base.rb

```
def deliver
  if valid?
    MailForm::Notifier.contact(self).deliver
  else
    false
  end
end
```

The class responsible for creating and delivering the email is MailForm::Notifier. Let's implement it using Action Mailer:

mail_form/5_delivery/lib/mail_form/notifier.rb

```
module MailForm
  class Notifier < ActionMailer::Base
    append_view_path File.expand_path("../../views", __FILE__)

    def contact(mail_form)
      @mail_form = mail_form
      mail(mail_form.headers)
    end
  end
end
```

The contact() action in our mailer assigns to @mail_form and then invokes the headers() method in the given Mail Form object. This method should return a hash with email data as keys like :to, :from, and :subject and should not be defined in MailForm::Base, but rather in each child class. This is a simple but powerful API contract that allows a developer to customize the email delivery without a need to redefine or monkey-patch the Notifier class.

Our MailForm::Notifier also calls append_view_path(), which adds lib/views inside our plug-in folder as a new location to search for templates. The last step before we run the test suite again is to autoload our new class:

mail_form/5_delivery/lib/mail_form.rb

```
autoload :Notifier, "mail_form/notifier"
```

Then let's define the headers() method in the SampleMail class:

mail_form/5_delivery/test/fixtures/sample_mail.rb

```
def headers
  { to: "recipient@example.com", from: self.email }
end
```

Now when we run rake test, it fails with the following message:

```
1) Failure:
test_delivers_an_email_with_attributes(MailFormTest):
ActionView::MissingTemplate: Missing template mail_form/notifier/contact
```

This is expected since we haven't added a template to our mailer. Our default mail template will show the message subject and print all attributes and their respective values:

```
mail_form/5_delivery/lib/views/mail_form/notifier/contact.text.erb
<%= message.subject %>
<% @mail_form.attribute_names.each do |key| -%>
  <%= @mail_form.class.human_attribute_name(key) %>: <%= @mail_form.send(key) %>
<% end -%>
```

To show all attributes, we need a list of all attribute names, but we don't keep such a list so far. We can implement such list by defining a class_attribute() called attributes_names() that is updated every time we call attributes():

```
mail_form/5_delivery/lib/mail_form/base.rb
# 1) Define a class attribute and initialize it
class_attribute :attribute_names
self.attribute_names = []

def self.attributes(*names)
  attr_accessor(*names)
  define_attribute_methods(names)

  # 2) Add new names as they are defined
  self.attribute_names += names
end
```

When we use class_attribute() for defining the names, it automatically works with inheritance. So if a class eventually inherits from our SampleMail fixture, it will automatically inherit all of its attribute names, too.

After we run rake test, all tests should be green again, and our Mail Form implementation is finished. Whenever we need to create a contact form, we create a class that inherits from MailForm::Base, we define our attributes and the email headers, and we're ready to go! To ensure it works exactly as we expect, let's check the whole process with an integration test.

2.2 Integration Tests with Capybara

In the previous chapter, we used Rails testing facilities to ensure a PDF was sent back to the client. To guarantee our project works as a contact form, we should create an actual form, submit it to the appropriate endpoint, and verify the email was sent. Those kind of tests are particularly hard to write using only the Rails testing tools. Most of the time, we end up writing direct requests to endpoints:

```
post "/contact_form", contact_form:
  { email: "jose@example.com", message: "hello"}
```

Writing a test using post() and explicit parameters is fine for some scenarios, particularly for APIs, but it falls flat when testing a contact-form workflow. For example, how do we guarantee there's a Submit button on the page? What happens when we click it? Is the request sent to the proper URL? What if we forget the email field?

To guarantee all those questions are answered, it's common to use a more robust testing tool like Capybara.[3] Capybara makes this sort of testing trivial by providing an easy-to-use domain-specific language (DSL), which we'll use throughout the book. The first step is to add it as a development dependency to our gemspec:

```
mail_form/5_delivery/mail_form.gemspec
s.add_development_dependency "capybara", "~> 2.0.0"
```

To use Capybara, let's define a brand-new test-case class called ActiveSupport::IntegrationCase. This class is built on top of ActiveSupport::TestCase and includes Rails's URL helpers and the Capybara DSL:

```
mail_form/5_delivery/test/test_helper.rb
require "capybara"
require "capybara/rails"

# Define a bare test case to use with Capybara
class ActiveSupport::IntegrationCase < ActiveSupport::TestCase
  include Capybara::DSL
  include Rails.application.routes.url_helpers
end
```

Now we're ready to write our first test using it:

```
mail_form/5_delivery/test/integration/navigation_test.rb
require "test_helper"

class NavigationTest < ActiveSupport::IntegrationCase
  setup do
    ActionMailer::Base.deliveries.clear
  end

  test "sends an e-mail after filling the contact form" do
    visit "/"

    fill_in "Name",    with: "John Doe"
    fill_in "Email",   with: "john.doe@example.com"
    fill_in "Message", with: "MailForm rocks!"

    click_button "Deliver"
```

---

3. https://github.com/jnicklas/capybara

```
    assert_match "Your message was successfully sent.", page.body

    assert_equal 1, ActionMailer::Base.deliveries.size
    mail = ActionMailer::Base.deliveries.last

    assert_equal ["john.doe@example.com"], mail.from
    assert_equal ["recipient@example.com"], mail.to
    assert_match "Message: MailForm rocks!", mail.body.encoded
  end
end
```

The integration test navigates to the root path, which returns a form with name, email, and message fields. On submitting the form, the server delivers an email to the configured recipient with the given message and shows the user a success message. To make the test pass, let's add the model, controller, views, and routes to our dummy app, starting with the routes:

mail_form/5_delivery/test/dummy/config/routes.rb
```
Dummy::Application.routes.draw do
  resources :contact_forms, only: :create
  root to: "contact_forms#new"
end
```

The controller and view follow:

mail_form/5_delivery/test/dummy/app/controllers/contact_forms_controller.rb
```
class ContactFormsController < ApplicationController
  def new
    @contact_form = ContactForm.new
  end

  def create
    @contact_form = ContactForm.new(params[:contact_form])

    if @contact_form.deliver
      redirect_to root_url, notice: "Your message was successfully sent."
    else
      render action: "new"
    end
  end
end
```

mail_form/5_delivery/test/dummy/app/views/contact_forms/new.html.erb
```
<h1>New Contact Form</h1>

<%= form_for(@contact_form) do |f| %>
  <% if @contact_form.errors.any? %>
  <div id="errorExplanation">
    <h2>Oops, something went wrong:</h2>
    <ul>
    <% @contact_form.errors.full_messages.each do |msg| %>
```

```
      <li><%= msg %></li>
    <% end %>
    </ul>
  </div>
  <% end %>
  <div class="field">
    <%= f.label :name %><br />
    <%= f.text_field :name %>
  </div>
  <div class="field">
    <%= f.label :email %><br />
    <%= f.text_field :email %>
  </div>
  <div class="field">
    <%= f.label :message %><br />
    <%= f.text_field :message %>
  </div>
  <div class="actions">
    <%= f.submit "Deliver" %>
  </div>
<% end %>
```

And finally, here's the model:

```
mail_form/5_delivery/test/dummy/app/models/contact_form.rb
class ContactForm < MailForm::Base
  attributes :name, :email, :message

  def headers
    { to: "recipient@example.com", from: self.email }
  end
end
```

Because our tests use flash messages, we need to add them to the layout just before the yield call:

```
mail_form/5_delivery/test/dummy/app/views/layouts/application.html.erb
<p style="color: green"><%= notice %></p>
```

With everything in place, let's run the test suite and...get an unexpected failure:

```
1) Error:
test_sends_an_e-mail_after_filling_the_contact_form(NavigationTest):
ArgumentError: wrong number of arguments (1 for 0)
  app/controllers/contact_forms_controller.rb:7:in `initialize'
```

The failure occurs because the initialize() method in MailForm::Base, unlike Active Record, does not expect a hash as an argument. Notice that an Active Model–compliant API does not say anything about how our models should be initialized. Let's implement an initialize() method, which receives a hash as an argument and sets attribute values:

```
mail_form/5_delivery/lib/mail_form/base.rb
def initialize(attributes = {})
  attributes.each do |attr, value|
    self.public_send("#{attr}=", value)
  end if attributes
end
```

After we define the previous method, our integration test succeeds, showing that everything works as expected. Remember that if you go to the dummy application inside test/dummy, you can run rails s as in any other Rails application. Feel free to start your server, add some validations to your ContactForm class, and have some fun with it.

2.3 Taking It to the Next Level

In the previous section, we wrote our Mail Form plug-in with some basic features and added integration testing to ensure it works. However, we can do a lot more with Active Model. Let's look at some examples.

Validators

Every Rails developer is familiar with Rails validations, as they are often used to exemplify the productivity that can be achieved with Rails. In the Rails source code, each validation is backed up by a *validator* class. Let's see the validates_presence_of() macro as an example:

```
rails/activemodel/lib/active_model/validations/presence.rb
def validates_presence_of(*attr_names)
  validates_with PresenceValidator, _merge_attributes(attr_names)
end
```

The validates_with() method is responsible for initializing the given ActiveModel::Validations::PresenceValidator class, and _merge_attributes() converts the given attributes to a hash. When you invoke the following

```
validates_presence_of :name
```

you're actually doing this:

```
validates_with PresenceValidator, attributes: [:name]
```

which is roughly the same as this:

```
validate PresenceValidator.new(attributes: [:name])
```

This process is similar to what happens with the validates() method:

```
validates :name, presence: true
```

This has the same effect as the following:

```
validate PresenceValidator.new(attributes: [:name])
```

The question is, how does Rails know that the :presence key should use the PresenceValidator? Simple: it converts the :presence key to "PresenceValidator" and then tries to find a constant named PresenceValidator in the current class, just like the following:

```
const_get("#{key.to_s.camelize}Validator")
```

This is important to discuss because now we can add any validator to any class, relying solely on Ruby's constant lookup. To understand exactly how it works, let's start a new irb session and type the following:

```
module Foo
  module Bar
  end
end

class Baz
  include Foo
end
```

```
Baz::Bar # => Foo::Bar
```

Notice how the last line of the script returns Foo::Bar even if Bar is not defined inside the Baz class. This happens because whenever a constant is looked up, Ruby searches inside all objects in the ancestor chain. Since Foo is included in Baz, Foo is an ancestor of Baz, allowing Ruby to find the Foo::Bar constant (you can check Baz ancestors by typing Baz.ancestors in the previous irb session).

To showcase how we can use this in practice, let's implement an absence validator in our MailForm::Base. Since a lot of spam usually comes through contact forms, we'll use the absence validator as a honey pot.

The honey pot works by creating a field, such as nickname, and hiding it with CSS. This way, humans do not see the field and consequently do not fill it in, but robots will fill it in like any other field. So whenever the nickname value is present, the email should not be sent because it is definitely spam.

Given Ruby's constant-lookup rules, we can add an :absence option to the validates() method of any class by implementing the AbsenceValidator inside a module and including this module in the desired class. Let's start by writing a simple test for it:

```
mail_form/6_final/test/mail_form_test.rb
test "validates absence of nickname" do
  sample = SampleMail.new(nickname: "Spam")
  assert !sample.valid?
  assert_equal ["is invalid"], sample.errors[:nickname]
end
```

The test shows the record must be invalid if the nickname field contains any value. Let's add the nickname field with :absence validation to our SampleMail object:

```
mail_form/6_final/test/fixtures/sample_mail.rb
attributes :nickname
validates :nickname, absence: true
```

When we run rake test, we get a test failure since SampleMail can no longer be loaded because AbsenceValidator is not defined anywhere. Let's create it:

```
mail_form/6_final/lib/mail_form/validators.rb
module MailForm
  module Validators
    class AbsenceValidator < ActiveModel::EachValidator
      def validate_each(record, attribute, value)
        record.errors.add(attribute, :invalid, options) unless value.blank?
      end
    end
  end
end
```

Our validator inherits from EachValidator. For every attribute given on initialization, EachValidator calls the validate_each() method with the record, the attribute, and its respective value. For each attribute, we add an error message unless the value is blank.

Next let's include MailForm::Validators in MailForm::Base:

```
mail_form/6_final/lib/mail_form/base.rb
include MailForm::Validators
```

This will add MailForm::Validators to the MailForm::Base ancestors chain. So, whenever we give :absence as a key to validates(), it will search for an AbsenceValidator constant, find it inside MailForm::Validators, and initialize it, similar to what it did with the PresenceValidator. To ensure it really works, we need to autoload our validators container:

```
mail_form/6_final/lib/mail_form.rb
autoload :Validators, 'mail_form/validators'
```

Run rake test, and all tests pass again. The beauty of this implementation is that adding the :absence key to validates() did not require us to register the option anywhere. Those options are discovered at runtime using Ruby's constant lookup.

Feel free to add the nickname field to our contact-form views and hide it with CSS, fully enabling our honey pot. It's up to you to write an integration test for it, since we still have some more Active Model investigation to do.

Callbacks

Wouldn't it be cool if we could provide hooks around the deliver() method so we could add some behavior *before* and *after* the delivery? This is quite easy to achieve with ActiveModel::Callbacks. To illustrate the API we intend to build, let's change our SampleMail fixture:

`mail_form/6_final/test/fixtures/sample_mail.rb`
```
before_deliver do
  evaluated_callbacks << :before
end
after_deliver do
  evaluated_callbacks << :after
end
def evaluated_callbacks
  @evaluated_callbacks ||= []
end
```

We have added an evaluated_callbacks() method to keep all evaluated callbacks and we implemented both before_deliver() and after_deliver() callbacks. Our test should call the deliver() in our SampleMail instance and assert both callbacks were evaluated:

`mail_form/6_final/test/mail_form_test.rb`
```
test "provides before and after deliver hooks" do
  sample = SampleMail.new(email: "user@example.com")
  sample.deliver
  assert_equal [:before, :after], sample.evaluated_callbacks
end
```

Finally, let's add support to callbacks in MailForm::Base. This can be done in three steps: extend our class with ActiveModel::Callbacks functionality, then define our callbacks, and finally overwrite deliver() implementation to run the callbacks before and after delivering:

`mail_form/6_final/lib/mail_form/base.rb`
```
# 1) Add callbacks behavior
extend ActiveModel::Callbacks

# 2) Define the callbacks. The line below will create both before_deliver
# and after_deliver callbacks with the same semantics as in Active Record
define_model_callbacks :deliver
```

```ruby
# 3) Change deliver to run the callbacks
def deliver
  if valid?
    run_callbacks(:deliver) do
      MailForm::Notifier.contact(self).deliver
    end
  else
    false
  end
end
```

As Active Record callbacks, you can give procs, strings, symbols, and any object that responds to the callback name. Feel free to try these options!

A Base Model

In many circumstances, a developer would like to achieve an Active Model–compliant API: in contact forms, when implementing search functionality, or even when splitting a sign-up flow into many steps. For this reason, Active Model provides an ActiveModel::Model module that can be included in any class:

```ruby
class Person
  include ActiveModel::Model
  attr_accessor :name, :age
end

person = Person.new(name: 'bob', age: '18')
person.name # => 'bob'
person.age  # => 18
```

By including ActiveModel::Model we are guaranteed that it will pass all ActiveModel::Lint::Tests tests. Let's take a look at its source:

```ruby
rails/activemodel/lib/active_model/model.rb
module ActiveModel
  module Model
    def self.included(base)
      base.class_eval do
        extend  ActiveModel::Naming
        extend  ActiveModel::Translation
        include ActiveModel::Validations
        include ActiveModel::Conversion
      end
    end

    def initialize(params={})
      params.each do |attr, value|
        self.public_send("#{attr}=", value)
      end if params
    end
```

```
    def persisted?
      false
    end
  end
end
```

As we can see, this basic module contains a subset of the behaviour we've implemented in this chapter. It's a good starting point whenever we need these functionalities in our applications!

2.4 Wrapping Up

In this chapter, we covered how to use Active Model to quickly create our own models that play seamlessly with Rails controllers and views. We talked about ActiveModel::AttributeMethods, ActiveModel::Conversion, ActiveModel::Naming, ActiveModel::Translation, ActiveModel::Validations, and finally ActiveModel::Callbacks. We also dove into Rails validators and how we can easily extend the validates() method behavior.

Even after all that, Active Model has a couple other modules to explore, like ActiveModel::Dirty and ActiveModel::Serialization. They let us bring dirty attributes and serializers such as to_xml() and to_json() right into our models, just like Active Record models.

Finally, if you enjoyed Mail Form here, check out the Mail Form by Plataformatec,[4] which is a production-ready gem created with the same concepts explored in this chapter. It also has additional features, such as attachment handling and the ability to append request information.

In the next chapter, we'll go back to studying the Rails rendering stack and extend it to look for a template in the database instead of the filesystem, keeping an eye on performance.

---

4. https://github.com/plataformatec/mail_form

In this chapter, we'll see
  • How to customize the Rails rendering stack to look up tem-
    plates from the database
  • How Ruby Hash lookup works
  • How to speed up controllers with ActionController::Metal

CHAPTER 3

Retrieving View Templates
from Custom Stores

When Rails renders a template, it has to get that template from somewhere. By default, Rails serves templates from the filesystem, but it doesn't need to be limited like that. Rails provides hooks that allow us to retrieve templates from anywhere we want, as long as we implement the required application programming interface (API). Let's explore this by building a mechanism that lets us serve templates from a database—templates that can be created, updated, and deleted through the web interface. But first let's take a deeper look at Rails's rendering stack.

3.1 Revisiting the Rendering Stack

In Section 1.3, *Understanding the Rails Rendering Stack*, on page 9, we saw that the main responsibility of the Rails controllers rendering stack is to normalize options and send them to an instance of ActionView::Renderer. When invoked, the renderer receives an instance of ActionView::Base called the view context, and a hash of normalized options used to find, compile, and render a specific template.

Whenever we render a template in Rails, its source must first be compiled into executable Ruby code. Every time some Ruby code is executed, its execution happens inside a given context and, in a Rails application, views are executed inside the view context object. All helpers available in our templates, such as form_for() and link_to(), are defined in modules included in the view context object.

Besides the view context, the view renderer has access to an instance of ActionView::LookupContext usually referred to as lookup_context. The *lookup context* is shared between controllers and views, and it holds all the information required to find a template. For example, whenever a JavaScript Object Notation (JSON) request comes, the request format is stored in the lookup_context object, so Rails will only look for templates tied to the JSON format.

The lookup context is also responsible for holding all view paths. A *view path* is a collection of objects able to find templates given a set of conditions. All controllers in a Rails application have one view path by default, which is a filesystem path pointing to app/views. Given a set of conditions like template name, locale, and format, this view path finds a specific template under app/views. For instance, whenever we have an HTML request at the index action of a UsersController, this default view path will attempt to pick a template at app/views/users/index.html.*. If the desired template is found, it's then compiled and rendered, as shown in the following image.

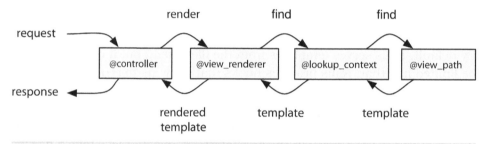

Figure 4—Rendering workflow between a controller, view renderer, lookup context, and view path

In *Delivering the Form*, on page 26, we manipulated the view path in our Mail-Form::Notifier object to include another path in the template lookup:

```
module MailForm
  class Notifier < ActionMailer::Base
    append_view_path File.expand_path("../../views", __FILE__)
  end
end
```

The preceding code states that if a template cannot be found under app/views, the mailer should look within the lib/views directory next.

Although we mostly set new view paths as strings, representing filesystem paths, Rails provides a well-defined API for adding any object as a view path. This means we're not forced to store view templates in the filesystem. We can store templates anywhere we want as long as we provide an object that knows how to find them. Although externally those objects are called view paths, internally Rails calls them *template resolvers*, and they must comply with the Resolver API.

Rails provides an abstract resolver implementation called ActionView::Resolver. In this chapter we'll use it to create a resolver that uses the database as a template store so we can store our pages in the database and edit them through a web interface using our favorite template handler (such as Liquid, ERB, or Haml). We can implement this functionality with one scaffold and a few lines of code!

3.2 Setting Up a SqlResolver

This time, instead of using rails plugin to implement the desired functionality, we'll develop the template-management system by building a Rails application called templater. Let's create it using the command line:

```
$ rails new templater
```

Next, let's define the model that will hold templates in the database using the Rails scaffold generator:

```
$ rails generate scaffold SqlTemplate body:text path:string \
    format:string locale:string handler:string partial:boolean
```

The body attribute is a text column used to store the whole template; the path should store a string similar to a filesystem path (for instance, the index() action under UsersController will have users/index as the path); format and locale hold the template format and its locale; the handler stores the template handler (for example, Liquid, ERB, or Haml); and, finally, partial tells us whether the stored template is a partial.

Before executing the generated migration, let's make one change in it, setting false as the default value for the partial attribute:

```
t.boolean :partial, default: false
```

And now we're ready to run our migrations:

```
$ bundle exec rake db:migrate
```

So far, no surprises. Next let's create a *template resolver*, which will use the SqlTemplate model to read templates from the database and expose them according to the Resolver API (described next).

The Resolver API

The Resolver API is composed of a single method, called find_all(), which should return an array of templates and has the following signature:

```
def find_all(name, prefix, partial, details, cache_key, locals)
```

For an HTML request at the index() action of a UsersController, those arguments are exactly as shown here:

```
find_all("index", "users", false, { formats: [:html],
  locale: [:en, :en], handlers: [:erb, :builder, :rjs] }, nil, [])
```

For this simple request, we can see that name maps to the action name, while prefix refers to the controller name. Next, partial is a Boolean that tells whether the template being rendered is a partial, and details is a hash with extra information for the lookup, such as the request formats, the current internationalization framework (I18n) locale followed by the default locale, and the available template handlers. The last two arguments are the cache_key (which we'll consider to be nil for now) and the locals variable (which is an empty array, as locals are used only when rendering a partial).

Rails provides an abstract resolver implementation, called ActionView::Resolver, which we'll use as the base for our resolver. Part of its source code is shown next, focusing on the find_all() and find_templates() methods:

```
rails/actionpack/lib/action_view/template/resolver.rb
module ActionView
  class Resolver
    cattr_accessor :caching
    self.caching = true

    def initialize
      @cache = Cache.new
    end

    def clear_cache
      @cache.clear
    end

    def find_all(name, prefix=nil, partial=false, details={}, key=nil, locals=[])
      cached(key, [name, prefix, partial], details, locals) do
        find_templates(name, prefix, partial, details)
      end
    end

    private

    def find_templates(name, prefix, partial, details)
      raise NotImplementedError
    end
  end
end
```

The find_all() method implements a basic caching mechanism where the block given to cached() is yielded only if no previous entry exists in the cache. When the block is invoked, it calls find_templates(), which raises a NotImplementedError, indicating it should be implemented in child classes. Notice that the cache_key and locals are used only by the cache mechanism; they are not passed down to template lookup.

Let's inherit from ActionView::Resolver and implement the find_templates() method using the SqlTemplate model to retrieve templates from the database, resulting in the same template lookup, as the next figure shows.

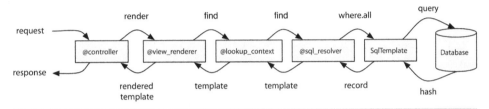

Figure 5—Template lookup with SqlTemplate

Writing the Code

Let's call our resolver implementation SqlTemplate::Resolver and implement it in three main steps. The first receives the name, prefix, partial, and details as arguments and normalizes them. Next, we create a SQL statement from the normalized arguments and query the database. The last step is to transform the array of records returned from the database into ActionView::Template instances.

Let's write a test first to demonstrate the functionality we want.

templater/1_resolver/test/models/sql_template_test.rb
```
require 'test_helper'

class SqlTemplateTest < ActiveSupport::TestCase
  test "resolver returns a template with the saved body" do
    resolver = SqlTemplate::Resolver.new
    details  = { formats: [:html], locale: [:en], handlers: [:erb] }

    # 1) Assert our resolver cannot find any template as the database is empty
    # find_all(name, prefix, partial, details)
    assert resolver.find_all("index", "posts", false, details).empty?

    # 2) Create a template in the database
    SqlTemplate.create!(
      body: "<%= 'Hi from SqlTemplate!' %>",
      path: "posts/index",
```

```
        format: "html",
        locale: "en",
        handler: "erb",
        partial: false)

    # 3) Assert that a template can now be found
    template = resolver.find_all("index", "posts", false, details).first
    assert_kind_of ActionView::Template, template

    # 4) Assert specific information about the found template
    assert_equal "<%= 'Hi from SqlTemplate!' %>", template.source
    assert_kind_of ActionView::Template::Handlers::ERB, template.handler
    assert_equal [:html], template.formats
    assert_equal "posts/index", template.virtual_path
    assert_match %r[SqlTemplate - \d+ - "posts/index"], template.identifier
  end
end
```

The find_all() method in our resolver should return an ActionView::Template instance. This template instance is initialized as follows:

```
ActionView::Template.new(source, identifier, handler, details)
```

The source is the body of the template stored in the database. The identifier is a unique string used to represent the template. We'll ensure its uniqueness by adding the template ID in the database.

The handler is the object responsible for compiling the template. The handler is not a string—like we stored in the database—but rather an object that's retrieved using the method registered_template_handler() from ActionView::Template:

```
ActionView::Template.registered_template_handler("erb") # =>
  #<ActionView::Template::Handlers::ERB:0x007fc722516490>
```

Finally, the last parameter given on template initialization is a hash with three keys: the :format of the template found, the last time the template was updated as :updated_at, and a :virtual_path that represents the template.

Since templates are no longer required to be in the filesystem, they do not necessarily have a path, and this breaks a couple of Rails features that depend explicitly on filesystem templates. One example is the I18n shortcut t(".message") inside your views. It uses the template filesystem path to retrieve the translation, so whenever you're inside a template at app/views/users/index, the shortcut attempts to find the I18n translation at "users.index.message".

To circumvent this need for a path, Rails requires templates to provide a :virtual_path. You can store your templates anywhere and give them any source or any identifier, but you need to provide a :virtual_path that represents what the path would be if this template were stored in the filesystem. This allows t(".message") to work as expected by setting the virtual path to users/index.

With tests in place and an understanding of how templates are initialized, let's implement our resolver by inheriting from ActionView::Resolver and implementing find_templates().

It's important to consider in our resolver that the order of the given details matters. In other words, if the locale array contains [:es, :en], a template in Spanish (:es) has higher preference than one in English if both exist. One solution is to generate an order clause for each detail and get the result properly sorted from the database. Another option is to sort the returned templates in Ruby. However, for simplicity, instead of passing all locales and formats to the SQL query, let's simply pick the first ones from the array.

Without further ado, let's implement our resolver:

```
templater/1_resolver/app/models/sql_template.rb
class SqlTemplate < ActiveRecord::Base
  validates :body, :path, presence: true
  validates :format,  inclusion: Mime::SET.symbols.map(&:to_s)
  validates :locale,  inclusion: I18n.available_locales.map(&:to_s)
  validates :handler, inclusion:
    ActionView::Template::Handlers.extensions.map(&:to_s)

  class Resolver < ActionView::Resolver
    protected

    def find_templates(name, prefix, partial, details)
      conditions = {
        path: normalize_path(name, prefix),
        locale: normalize_array(details[:locale]).first,
        format: normalize_array(details[:formats]).first,
        handler: normalize_array(details[:handlers]),
        partial: partial || false
      }
      ::SqlTemplate.where(conditions).map do |record|
        initialize_template(record)
      end
    end
    # Normalize name and prefix, so the tuple ["index", "users"] becomes
    # "users/index" and the tuple ["template", nil] becomes "template".
    def normalize_path(name, prefix)
      prefix.present? ? "#{prefix}/#{name}" : name
    end
    # Normalize arrays by converting all symbols to strings.
    def normalize_array(array)
      array.map(&:to_s)
    end
```

```ruby
    # Initialize an ActionView::Template object based on the record found.
    def initialize_template(record)
      source = record.body
      identifier = "SqlTemplate - #{record.id} - #{record.path.inspect}"
      handler = ActionView::Template.registered_template_handler(record.handler)

      details = {
        format: Mime[record.format],
        updated_at: record.updated_at,
        virtual_path: virtual_path(record.path, record.partial)
      }
      ActionView::Template.new(source, identifier, handler, details)
    end

    # Make paths as "users/user" become "users/_user" for partials.
    def virtual_path(path, partial)
      return path unless partial
      if index = path.rindex("/")
        path.insert(index + 1, "_")
      else
        "_#{path}"
      end
    end
  end
end
```

Our implementation normalizes the given arguments, queries the database, and creates template objects from the result set. We also added several validations to our model, ensuring the body and path values cannot be blank, and guaranteeing a valid format, locale, and handler are supplied.

As a result of adding some validations to our models, some functional tests are failing since our fixtures now contain invalid data. To make them pass, let's change the fixture at test/fixtures/sql_templates.yml to include a valid format, locale, and handler:

templater/1_resolver/test/fixtures/sql_templates.yml

```yaml
one:
  id: 1
  path: "some/path"
  format: "html"
  locale: "en"
  handler: "erb"
  partial: false
  body: "Body"
```

Now with our resolver implemented and a green test suite, we get to create a new scaffold and make it use templates from the database instead of the filesystem. Let's create a user scaffold by running the following command:

```
$ rails generate scaffold User name:string
```

We'll run our migrations next:

```
$ bundle exec rake db:migrate
```

We can now start the server, access /users, and perform all create, read, update, and delete operations as usual.

Next let's access the /sql_templates path and create a new template by filling the template body with the same contents as the file in app/views/users/index.html.erb; setting the path with users/index; setting the format, locale, and handler to html, en, and erb, respectively; and keeping the Partial box unchecked.

Save this new template and head back to the /users path. Now delete the view file app/views/users/index.html.erb, and rerender the page. You should get a "Template is missing" error, but don't worry, because we expect that. The template is stored in the database, but we still haven't told the UsersController to use our new resolver to retrieve it.

Let's do that by adding the following line to UsersController:

```
templater/1_resolver/app/controllers/users_controller.rb
class UsersController < ApplicationController
  append_view_path SqlTemplate::Resolver.new
```

When we refresh the page at /users, we see the whole index page once again retrieved from the database! And although the template is in the database, the layout still comes from the filesystem. In other words, in a single request we can get templates from different resolvers in our view paths.

Feel free to head back to /sql_templates, manipulate the body of the stored template, and notice that the index() action in the UsersController will change accordingly. The fact that we can achieve this behavior in so few lines of code shows the power of the ActionView::Resolver abstraction.

Before we move to the next section, let's run the test suite once again. A test is failing with an error message:

```
1) Error:
test_should_get_index(UsersControllerTest)
ActionView::MissingTemplate: Missing template users/index,
  application/index with {:locale=>[:en], :formats=>[:html],
  :handlers=>[:erb, :builder, :raw, :ruby, :jbuilder, :coffee]}. Searched in:
  * "templater/app/views"
  * "#<SqlTemplate::Resolver:0x007f9774fbc0d0>"
```

This happens because we deleted the template from the filesystem. Although we added the same template to our development database, our test database remains clean, raising this MissingTemplate error in the test environment. To fix this, let's change our sql_templates fixture.

```
templater/1_resolver/test/fixtures/sql_templates.yml
users_index:
  id: 2
  path: "users/index"
  format: "html"
  locale: "en"
  handler: "erb"
  partial: false
  body: "<h1>Listing users</h1>
<table>
  <tr>
    <th>Name</th>
    <th></th>
    <th></th>
    <th></th>
  </tr>
<%% @users.each do |user| %>
  <tr>
    <td><%%= user.name %></td>
    <td><%%= link_to 'Show', user %></td>
    <td><%%= link_to 'Edit', edit_user_path(user) %></td>
    <td><%%= link_to 'Destroy', user,
        data: { confirm: 'Are you sure?' }, method: :delete %></td>
  </tr>
<%% end %>
</table>
<br />
<%%= link_to 'New user', new_user_path %>"
```

Our fixture is just a copy of the template. The only caveat is that Rails parses fixtures with ERB, so we need to escape our ERB tags using <%% ... %>. And that's all—our tests are all green again.

3.3 Configuring Our Resolver for Production

To ensure the template lookup is fast in production, Rails provides some caching conveniences. Let's explore those conveniences so we understand how to enable caching for our templates, and the strategies available to us to expire this cache whenever a template is saved to the database.

As mentioned earlier, Rails gives our resolver a cache_key through the find_all() method. Our first stop is to learn why Rails creates this cache key and how our resolver uses it.

The Resolvers Cache

As we saw in the code on page 42, ActionView::Resolver's find_all() method automatically caches templates using the cached() method. The cache is created on initialization and referenced by the instance variable @cached. The resolver caches templates only if Rails.application.config.cache_classes returns true; additionally, it exposes a clear_cache() method to clear its cache.

Each template must be cached in a function of five values: the cache_key, its prefix, its name, whether it is a partial or not, and the set of locals. Given those five keys, we could store the templates in the cache in these three ways:

```
# Nested hash
@cached[key][prefix][name][partial][locals]

# Simple hash with array as key
@cached[[key, prefix, name, partial, locals]]

# Simple hash with hash as key
@cached[key: key, prefix: prefix, name: name, partial: partial, locals: locals]
```

All three cache implementations give us the desired behavior. However, there is a difference between them: performance. We need to explore how Ruby does hash lookups to understand this.

Ruby Hash Lookup

Whenever we store a value for a given key in a Hash object, Ruby stores three things: the given key, the given value, and the object hash for the given key. This hash is the result of the Object#hash() method called on the object given as the key. There is an easy way to prove that Ruby Hash in fact relies on Object#hash(); just start an irb session, and type the following:

```
class NoHash
  undef_method :hash
end

hash = Hash.new
hash[NoHash.new] = 1
# => NoMethodError: undefined method `hash' for #<NoHash:0x101643820>
```

If we undefine the hash() method in our object, it can no longer be stored in the hash. Adding an element to the hash is similar to creating a new entry in a table, as shown in Figure 6, *Illustration of what a hash stores for each entry*, on page 50.

Whenever we attempt to retrieve the value for a given key in a Hash object, like hash[:b], Ruby calculates the Object#hash() for this given key and then searches

① hash = {}

Hash	Key	Value

② hash[:a] = 1

Hash	Key	Value
363868	:a	1

③ hash[:b] = 2

Hash	Key	Value
363868	:a	1
231228	:b	2

④ hash[:c] = 3

Hash	Key	Value
363868	:a	1
231228	:b	2
231388	:c	3

Figure 6—Illustration of what a hash stores for each entry. Keep in mind the Ruby implementation uses pointers instead of a table structure, but the table is an easy way to represent how it works.

whether one or more entries in the Hash object have this same hash value. For instance, the value returned by :b.hash is 231228 in the preceding figure. Seeing that one or more entries have the value 231228, Ruby checks whether any key for these entries is equal to the given key, using the equality operator eql?(). Since :b.eql?(:b) returns true, accessing hash[:b] in our example successfully returns 2 as the result.

To prove that Ruby uses Object#hash() to localize entries, let's start another irb session and do a few experiments.

```
hash   = {}
object = Object.new
hash[object] = 1
hash[object] # => 1

def object.hash; 123; end

hash[object] # => nil
hash         # => {#<Object:0x1016e3de8>=>1}
```

This time we used an arbitrary Ruby object as a hash key, and we could successfully set and get values. However, after we modified the value object#hash returned, the value could not be found even though the same object is still in the hash.

Ruby stores Object#hash() for each key to provide faster lookups. Comparing hash values (integers) is much faster than comparing each object stored in the hash.

This implementation implies that the performance hit of finding a value in the hash is not merely in the eql?() method, but also in calculating Object#hash() for the given key. Remember, we could implement our resolver cache using a nested hash or a simple hash with arrays as the key, or a simple hash with hashes as keys. We should choose the first, because in the nested-hash case, the hash keys are strings or Booleans, and Ruby knows how to calculate the Object#hash() value for these very quickly. On the other hand, calculating Object#hash() and equality for arrays and hashes is more expensive.

We can demonstrate this in another irb session:

```
require "benchmark"
foo     = "foo"
bar     = "bar"
array   = [foo, bar]
hash    = {a: foo, b: bar}

nested_hash = Hash.new { |h,k| h[k] = {} }
nested_hash[foo][bar] = true

array_hash = { array => true }
hash_hash  = { hash => true }

Benchmark.realtime { 1000.times { nested_hash[foo][bar] } } # => 0.000342
Benchmark.realtime { 1000.times { array_hash[array] } }     # => 0.000779
Benchmark.realtime { 1000.times { hash_hash[hash] } }       # => 0.001645
```

The nested-hash implementation yields better results. Although the choice for a nested hash *apparently* does not yield substantial gains, the concepts we covered about Hash lookups in Ruby are fundamental to understanding the next section.

The Cache Key

We already know that our resolvers come with a built-in cache. We also know that this cache uses a nested hash to store templates and that the cache depends on five values: @cached[key][prefix][name][partial][locals]. However, the find_all() signature receives six arguments:

```
def find_all(name, prefix=nil, partial=false, details={}, key=nil, locals=[])
```

details is a hash containing the format, locale, and other information useful for the template lookup. The *lookup context* holds this information, and it is essential for retrieving the correct template from the filesystem. So why doesn't the cache use these details?

Remember how we determined that calculating the Object#hash() for a hash object is expensive when compared to simpler structures, like strings? If we were to use details as the key in the cache's nested hash, it would be slow since details is a hash of arrays:

```
details # => {
  formats: [:html],
  locale: [:en, :en],
  handlers: [:erb, :builder, :rjs]
}

# Slow because details is a hash of arrays
@cached[details][prefix][name][partial][locals]
```

Instead, the lookup context generates a simple Ruby object for each details hash and sends it as cache_key to resolvers. The whole process is similar to the following code:

```
# Generate an object for the details hash
@details_key ||= {}
key = @details_key[details] ||= Object.new

# And send it to each resolver
resolver.find_all(name, prefix, partial, details, key)

# Inside the resolver, the details value is not used in the cache
# Instead we use the key, which is a simple object and fast
@cached[key][prefix][name][partial][locals]
```

In other words, details is not used directly in the cache, but rather via the cache_key. This is important because during a request the details hash rarely changes, as the format and locale are usually set before rendering any template. Therefore, regardless of how many templates are rendered and resolvers are involved in a request, the cache_key is likely to be calculated just once. If a detail changes, such as the request format, a new cache_key is generated.

Let's fire up irb once again and do our last benchmark in this chapter. Our benchmark will show how accessing a hash using a simple Object, like the cache_key, compares with using a hash of arrays, like the details hash:

```
require "benchmark"
cache_key = Object.new
details   = {
```

```
    formats:  [:html, :xml, :json],
    locale:   [:en],
    handlers: [:erb, :builder, :rjs]
}

hash_1 = { cache_key => 10 }
hash_2 = { details => 10 }

Benchmark.realtime { 1000.times { hash_1[cache_key] } } # => 0.000202
Benchmark.realtime { 1000.times { hash_2[details] } }   # => 0.003937
```

Twenty times slower is quite a difference! For applications that require high performance, these milliseconds can easily mount up in requests that render several collections and partials, dramatically affecting the response time. In some benchmarks done with Rails, using the details hash *took up to ten percent of the time spent in the rendering stack*, while using the cache_key reduced this to less than one percent.

Expiring the Cache

Since Rails automatically handles the cache inside resolvers, we only need to worry about expiring the cache using the Resolver#clear_cache() method. This cache is stored in the resolver instance, so to expire these caches, we would need to track all instances of SqlTemplate::Resolver and call clear_cache() in each of them whenever we add or update a template in the database.

However, does it make sense to create several SqlTemplate::Resolver instances? Because the cache is in the instance, creating several instances would create several caches, reducing their effectiveness. Therefore, we don't want several resolver instances. We want only one shared across the entire application.

We need a *singleton* class. Luckily, Ruby has a Singleton module in its Standard Library, which does all the hard work for us. Including this module in SqlTemplate::Resolver makes SqlTemplate::Resolver.new() a private method and exposes SqlTemplate::Resolver.instance() instead, which always returns the same object.

Also, having a singleton object makes it very easy to expire the cache. Since we can always access the instantiated resolver with SqlTemplate::Resolver.instance(), we just need to call clear_cache() on it every time we save a SqlTemplate instance.

Let's get started with those changes. The first one is to require and include Singleton inside SqlTemplate::Resolver:

templater/2_improving/app/models/sql_template.rb
```
require "singleton"
include Singleton
```

After doing this simple change, we need to update both app/controllers/users_controller.rb and test/models/sql_template_test.rb to call SqlTemplate::Resolver.instance() instead of SqlTemplate::Resolver.new():

```
templater/2_improving/app/controllers/users_controller.rb
append_view_path SqlTemplate::Resolver.instance
```

```
templater/2_improving/test/models/sql_template_test.rb
resolver = SqlTemplate::Resolver.instance
```

With our singleton resolver in place, let's write a test in test/models/sql_template_test.rb that asserts that our cache is properly expired. This new test should update the SqlTemplate from fixtures and assert that our resolver will return the updated template:

```
templater/2_improving/test/models/sql_template_test.rb
test "sql_template expires the cache on update" do
  cache_key = Object.new
  resolver  = SqlTemplate::Resolver.instance
  details   = { formats: [:html], locale: [:en], handlers: [:erb] }

  t = resolver.find_all("index", "users", false, details, cache_key).first
  assert_match "Listing users", t.source

  sql_template = sql_templates(:users_index)
  sql_template.update_attributes(body: "New body for template")

  t = resolver.find_all("index", "users", false, details, cache_key).first
  assert_equal "New body for template", t.source
end
```

Notice we generated a fake cache_key with Object.new to pass to find_all() because the cache is activated only if a cache key is supplied.

Finally, to make our test pass, let's add an after_save callback to SqlTemplate, right after the model validations:

```
templater/2_improving/app/models/sql_template.rb
after_save do
  SqlTemplate::Resolver.instance.clear_cache
end
```

Now every time a template is created or updated, the cache is expired, allowing the modified template to be picked up and recompiled. Unfortunately, this approach has a severe limitation: it works for only single-instance deployments. For example, if your infrastructure contains more than one server or if you use Passenger or Unicorn with a pool of instances, a request will reach a specific instance, which will have only its own cache cleared up. In other words, this cache is not synchronized between machines.

Luckily, we can solve this issue:

- One option is to reimplement the cache using memcached or Redis so it is shared between machines with an appropriate expiration mechanism.[1,2]

- Another option is to notify each instance whenever the cache is expired —for example, through a queue. In this schema, after_save() would simply push a message to the queue, which would send a notification to all subscribed instances.

- We can also solve this by setting config.action_view.cache_template_loading to false on production. Previously I mentioned that the resolver cache is enabled only if config.cache_classes is true.

  However, whenever cache_template_loading() is set, it has higher preference than the cache_classes() configuration. If the template cache is disabled, Rails queries the database every time a template lookup happens, but the template is recompiled only if the updated_at value we set on template creation is more recent than the one the resolver has cached. So, even though we trigger a new query, the expensive template compilation happens only if needed. This is how Rails behaves by default in development.

Which strategy is best for you depends on your infrastructure, performance requirements, and how frequently templates are changed.

With that, we've finished our SqlTemplate::Resolver implementation!

3.4 Serving Templates with Metal

Now that we can create and edit templates from the UI and serve them with our own resolver, we're ready to take it to the next level. Let's use our templater tooling as a simple content-management system (CMS).

Creating the CmsController

We already can create, update, and delete templates by accessing /sql_templates; now we need to expose them depending on the accessed URL.

To achieve this, let's map all requests under /cms/* to a controller that will use our resolver to find the template in the database, and render them back to the client. A request at /cms/about should render a SqlTemplate stored in the database with path equals to about.

---

1. http://memcached.org/
2. http://redis.io

We can implement this functionality with a few lines of code. Let's start with an integration test that we'll write using Capybara. The first step is to set up Capybara as we did in Section 2.2, *Integration Tests with Capybara*, on page 28:

templater/2_improving/test/test_helper.rb

```ruby
require "capybara"
require "capybara/rails"

# Define a bare test case to use with Capybara
class ActiveSupport::IntegrationCase < ActiveSupport::TestCase
  include Capybara::DSL
  include Rails.application.routes.url_helpers
end
```

Add it as a dependency to the Gemfile:

templater/2_improving/Gemfile

```ruby
group :test do
  gem 'capybara', '~> 2.0.0'
end
```

Finally, write the test that creates a template and renders it:

templater/2_improving/test/integration/cms_test.rb

```ruby
require 'test_helper'

class CmsTest < ActiveSupport::IntegrationCase
  test "can access any page in SqlTemplate" do
    visit "/sql_templates"
    click_link "New Sql template"

    fill_in "Body",    with: "My first CMS template"
    fill_in "Path",    with: "about"
    fill_in "Format",  with: "html"
    fill_in "Locale",  with: "en"
    fill_in "Handler", with: "erb"

    click_button "Create Sql template"
    assert_match "Sql template was successfully created.", page.body

    visit "/cms/about"
    assert_match "My first CMS template", page.body
  end
end
```

To make our new test pass, let's write a route that will map to our CmsController:

templater/2_improving/config/routes.rb

```ruby
get "cms/*page", to: "cms#respond"
```

This route maps all requests at /cms/* to the respond() action in the CmsController, which we implement as follows:

```
templater/2_improving/app/controllers/cms_controller.rb
class CmsController < ApplicationController
  prepend_view_path SqlTemplate::Resolver.instance

  def respond
    render template: params[:page]
  end
end
```

We simply pass the given route as a template name, which is forwarded to our SqlTemplate::Resolver that looks up the template. Notice we prepend our resolver to the view paths this time, as it is the main source for templates. Our test suite is green again!

If you want to test our simple CMS manually, fire up the server, go to /sql_templates, create a new template with path equal to about, and add some content. Then access /cms/about and see your new page!

Playing with Metal

Our CmsController inherits from ApplicationController, which inherits from ActionController::Base, and consequently it comes with all the functionality available in regular Rails controllers. It includes all helpers, adds cross-site request forgery protection, allows us to hide actions with hide_action(), supports flash messages, and adds the respond_to() method—it does a lot more than required since our controller handles only GET requests. Wouldn't it be nice if we could somehow have a simpler controller, with just the behavior we need?

We've already discussed Abstract Controller and how it provides a basic structure that is shared between Action Mailer and Action Controller. However, AbstractController::Base doesn't know anything about HTTP. On the other hand, ActionController::Base comes with the whole package. Isn't there a point in the middle?

Indeed there is! It's called ActionController::Metal. ActionController::Metal inherits from AbstractController::Base and implements the minimum functionality required for our controllers to be a valid Rack application and work with HTTP. The inheritance chain is as shown in Figure 7, *CmsController superclasses*, on page 58.

By taking a quick look at ActionController::Base in the Rails source code, we notice it inherits from Metal and adds a bunch of behavior:

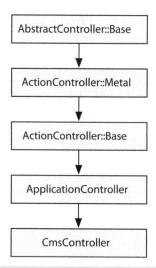

Figure 7—CmsController superclasses

rails/actionpack/lib/action_controller/base.rb

```
module ActionController
  class Base < Metal
    abstract!

    include AbstractController::Layouts
    include AbstractController::Translation
    include AbstractController::AssetPaths
    include Helpers
    include HideActions
    include UrlFor
    include Redirecting
    include Rendering
    include Renderers::All
    include ConditionalGet
    include RackDelegation
    include Caching
    include MimeResponds
    include ImplicitRender
    include StrongParameters
    include Cookies
    include Flash
    include RequestForgeryProtection
    include ForceSSL
    include Streaming
    include DataStreaming
    include RecordIdentifier
    include HttpAuthentication::Basic::ControllerMethods
    include HttpAuthentication::Digest::ControllerMethods
```

```
    include HttpAuthentication::Token::ControllerMethods
    include AbstractController::Callbacks
    include Rescue
    include Instrumentation
    include ParamsWrapper

    ActiveSupport.run_load_hooks(:action_controller, self)
  end
end
```

Let's reimplement CmsController, but this time we'll inherit from ActionController::Metal and include only the modules we need, which reduces the overhead in a request:

templater/3_final/app/controllers/cms_controller.rb
```
class CmsController < ActionController::Metal
  include ActionController::Rendering
  include AbstractController::Helpers
  prepend_view_path ::SqlTemplate::Resolver.instance
  helper CmsHelper

  def respond
    render template: params[:page]
  end
end

module CmsHelper
end
```

After these changes, our tests should still be green, showing that our new controller implementation using ActionController::Metal works as expected.

If we need more functionality, we add the required modules. For instance, if we want to add layouts, we include the AbstractController::Layouts module, create a layout in the database with the path layouts/cms, and specify layout "cms" in the controller. Try it!

3.5   Wrapping Up

We've covered a lot in this chapter. We analyzed Action View's rendering stack and developed a resolver that reads templates from a database with cache-expiration mechanisms. Then we created a controller to dynamically access the pages in the resolver and optimized it by making it an ActionController::Metal object. If you're eager to see more examples of using resolvers, check the Rails source code and discover how it implements the filesystem resolver, which retrieves templates from the filesystem.[3]

---

3.   https://github.com/rails/rails/blob/4-0-stable/actionpack/lib/action_view/template/resolver.rb

On the other hand, if you're already familiar with Rails's internals (such as resolvers and metal) and are still looking for a challenge, you can learn more about Ruby hashes by checking the Rubinius source code. Rubinius implements most of the Ruby language in Ruby itself, including the Hash class, so you can learn a lot by looking through its source code.[4]

In the next chapter, we'll discuss template handlers such as ERB, Builder, and Haml. We'll create our own handler using Markdown and ERB, and we'll hook it into Rails's generators.

---

4.   https://github.com/rubinius/rubinius/blob/v2.1.0/kernel/common/hash.rb

In this chapter, we'll see
- The Rails template-handler API
- Multipart templates with Action Mailer
- Rails generators and railties

## CHAPTER 4

Sending Multipart Emails Using Template Handlers

To finish our tour of the Rails rendering stack, let's look at how Rails compiles and renders templates. So far, we've seen that a controller's responsibility is to normalize the rendering options and send them to the view renderer. Based on these options, the view renderer asks the lookup context to search for a specific template in the available resolvers, also taking into account the locale and format values the lookup context holds.

As we saw in *Writing the Code*, on page 43, the resolver returns instances of ActionView::Template, and at the moment those instances are initialized, we need to pass along an object called handler as an argument. Each extension, such as .erb or .haml, has its own template handler:

```
ActionView::Template.registered_template_handler("erb")
  #=> #<ActionView::Template::Handlers::ERB:0x007fc722516490>
```

The *template handler*'s responsibility in the rendering stack is to compile a template to Ruby source code. This source code is executed inside the view context and must return the rendered template as a string. Figure 8, *Objects involved in the rendering stack*, on page 62 summarizes this process.

To understand how a template handler works, we'll build a template handler to solve a particular issue. Even though the foundation for today's emails was created in 1970 and version 4 of the HTML specification dates from 1997, we still cannot rely on sending HTML emails to everyone since many email clients can't render these properly.

This implies that whenever we configure an application to send an HTML email, we should also send a plain-text version of the same, creating a "mul-

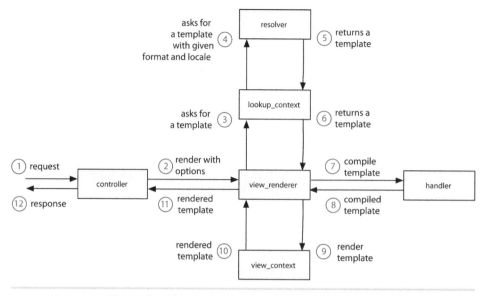

Figure 8—Objects involved in the rendering stack

tipart" email. If the email's recipient uses a client that cannot read HTML, it will fall back to the plain-text part.

Action Mailer makes creating multipart emails a breeze, but with this approach we have to maintain two versions of the same email message. Wouldn't it be nice if we had one template that could be rendered both as plain text and as HTML?

Here's where Markdown comes in. Markdown is a lightweight markup language, created by John Gruber and Aaron Swartz, that is intended to be as easy as possible to read and write.[1] Markdown's syntax consists entirely of punctuation characters and allows you to embed custom HTML whenever required. Here's an example of Markdown text:

```
Welcome
=======

Hi, José Valim!

Thanks for choosing our product. Before you use it, you just need
to confirm your account by accessing the following link:

http://example.com/confirmation?token=ASDFGHJK
```

---

1. http://daringfireball.net/projects/markdown

```
Remember, you have *7 days* to confirm it. For more information,
you can visit our [FAQ][1] or our [Customer Support page][2].


Regards,

The Team.

[1]: http://example.com/faq
[2]: http://example.com/customer
```

Indeed, it's quite readable! The best part is that it can be transformed into HTML, which is rendered as shown in the following figure.

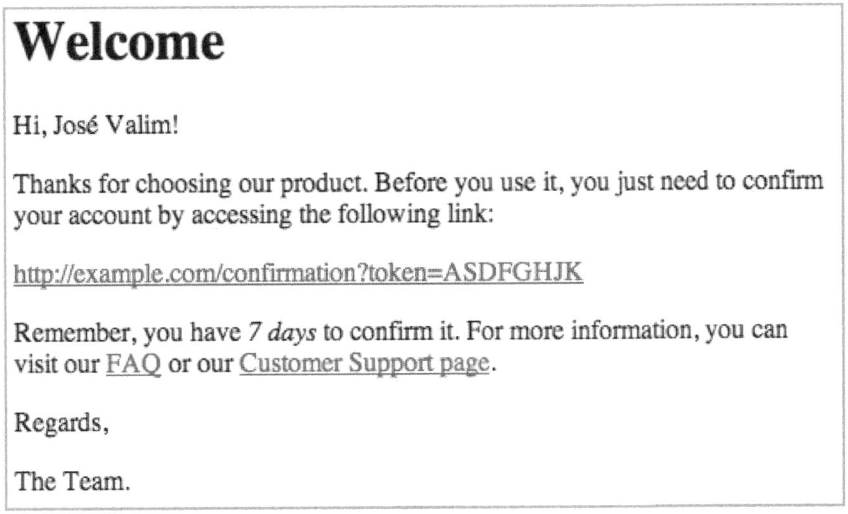

Figure 9—HTML generated from a Markdown template

Our template handler will use Markdown's features to generate both plain-text and HTML views using just one template. The only issue with Markdown is that it does not interpret Ruby code. To circumvent this, we must compile our templates with ERB and then convert them using the Markdown compiler.

At the end of this chapter, we'll hook into Rails's generators and configure the mailer generator to use our new template handler by default.

4.1 Playing with the Template-Handler API

For an object to be compliant with the handler API, it needs to respond to the call() method. This method receives as an argument an instance of ActionView::Template, which we introduced in *Writing the Code*, on page 43, and should return a string containing valid Ruby code. The Ruby code the handler returns is then compiled into a method, so rendering a template is as simple as invoking this compiled method.

Before diving into our Markdown + ERB handler, let's create a few template handlers to get acquainted with the API.

Ruby Template Handler

Our first template handler simply allows arbitrary Ruby code as a template. This means the following template is valid:

```
body = ""
body << "This is my first "
body << content_tag(:b, "template handler")
body << "!"
body
```

To implement this, let's craft a new plug-in called handlers using rails plugin:

```
$ rails plug-in new handlers
```

Next, let's write a simple integration test for our template handler. Our goal is to render a dummy template at test/dummy/app/views/handlers/rb_handler.html.rb:

```
handlers/1_first_handlers/test/dummy/app/views/handlers/rb_handler.html.rb
body = ""
body << "This is my first "
body << content_tag(:b, "template handler")
body << "!"
body
```

Our integration test will need routes and a controller to serve that template, so let's add them:

```
handlers/1_first_handlers/test/dummy/config/routes.rb
Dummy::Application.routes.draw do
  get "/handlers/:action", to: "handlers"
end
```

```
handlers/1_first_handlers/test/dummy/app/controllers/handlers_controller.rb
class HandlersController < ApplicationController
end
```

Our integration test should make a request to the defined route at /handlers/rb_handler and assert our template was properly rendered:

```
handlers/1_first_handlers/test/integration/rendering_test.rb
require "test_helper"

class RenderingTest < ActionDispatch::IntegrationTest
  test ".rb template handler" do
    get "/handlers/rb_handler"
```

```
    expected = "This is my first <b>template handler</b>!"
    assert_match expected, response.body
  end
end
```

When we run the test suite, it fails because Rails still does not recognize the .rb extension in templates. To register a new template handler, we invoke ActionView::Template.register_template_handler() with two arguments: the template extension and the handler object. Because the handler object is anything that responds to call() and returns a String, we can implement our handler simply using Ruby's lambda:

```
handlers/1_first_handlers/lib/handlers.rb
require "action_view/template"
ActionView::Template.register_template_handler :rb,
  lambda { |template| template.source }
module Handlers
end
```

When we run the test suite, the test we just wrote now passes. Our lambda receives an ActionView::Template instance as an argument. Since our template handler needs to return a String with Ruby code and our template in the filesystem is written in Ruby, we just need to return the template.source().

As Ruby symbols implement a to_proc() method and :source.to_proc is exactly the same as lambda { |arg| arg.source }, we can make our template handler even shorter:

```
ActionView::Template.register_template_handler :rb, :source.to_proc
```

String Template Handler

Our .rb template handler is quite simple but has limited usage. Rails views usually have big chunks of static contents, and handling those in the Ruby code would quickly become messy. That said, let's implement another template handler that is more suited to handling static content but that still allows us to embed Ruby code. Since strings in Ruby support interpolation, our next template handler will be based on Ruby strings. Let's add a sample template to the dummy app:

```
handlers/1_first_handlers/test/dummy/app/views/handlers/string_handler.html.string
Congratulations! You just created another #{@what}!
```

Our new template uses string interpolation, and the interpolated Ruby code references an instance variable named @what. Let's define a new action with this instance variable in our HandlersController for our tests to use as a fixture:

handlers/1_first_handlers/test/dummy/app/controllers/handlers_controller.rb
```
class HandlersController < ApplicationController
  def string_handler
    @what = "template handler"
  end
end
```

Now let's write a small test for it in our integration suite:

handlers/1_first_handlers/test/integration/rendering_test.rb
```
test ".string template handler" do
  get "/handlers/string_handler"
  expected = "Congratulations! You just created another template handler!"
  assert_match expected, response.body
end
```

To make our new test pass, let's implement this new template handler, once again in lib/handlers.rb:

handlers/1_first_handlers/lib/handlers.rb
```
ActionView::Template.register_template_handler :string,
  lambda { |template| "%Q{#{template.source}}" }
```

Run the test suite, and our new test passes. Our template handler returns a string created with the Ruby shortcut %Q{}, which Rails then compiles to a method. When this method is invoked, the Ruby interpreter evaluates the string and returns the interpolated result.

This template handler works fine for simple cases, but has two major flaws: adding the } character to the template causes syntax errors unless the character is escaped, and the block support is limited because it needs to be wrapped in the whole interpolation syntax. That means both of the following examples are invalid:

```
This } causes a syntax error
```

```
#{2.times do}
  This does not work as in ERB and is invalid
#{end}
```

So it's time to look at more-robust template handlers.

4.2 Building a Template Handler with Markdown + ERB

Several gems can compile Markdown syntax to HTML. For our template handler, let's use RDiscount,[2] which is a Ruby wrapper to the fast Markdown compiler library called Discount, written in C.

---

2. https://github.com/rtomayko/rdiscount

Markdown Template Handler

We can create a template handler that compiles to Markdown in just a couple lines of code. Let's first add another test to our suite:

```
handlers/1_first_handlers/test/integration/rendering_test.rb
test ".md template handler" do
  get "/handlers/rdiscount"
  expected = "<p>RDiscount is <em>cool</em> and <strong>fast</strong>!</p>"
  assert_match expected, response.body
end
```

And then let's write our template in the filesystem:

```
handlers/1_first_handlers/test/dummy/app/views/handlers/rdiscount.html.md
RDiscount is *cool* and **fast**!
```

Note that our template uses .md as the extension for Markdown. Let's register it in Rails:

```
handlers/1_first_handlers/lib/handlers.rb
require "rdiscount"
ActionView::Template.register_template_handler :md,
  lambda { |template| "RDiscount.new(#{template.source.inspect}).to_html" }
```

Since our template handler relies on RDiscount, let's add it as a dependency to our plug-in and run bundle install just afterward:

```
handlers/1_first_handlers/handlers.gemspec
s.add_dependency "rdiscount", "~> 2.0.0"
```

When we run the test suite, our new test passes. Our Markdown template handler works like a charm, but it doesn't allow us to embed Ruby code, so its usage becomes quite limited.

To circumvent this limitation, we could use the same technique we used in our .string template handler, but it also has limitations. Therefore, we'll use ERB to embed Ruby code in our Markdown template and create a new template handler named .merb.

MERB Template Handler

First let's add an example of our new template handler to the filesystem. This example should be inside our dummy app, and we'll use it in our tests:

```
handlers/1_first_handlers/test/dummy/app/views/handlers/merb.html.merb
MERB template handler is **<%= %w(cool fast).to_sentence %>**!
```

And then let's write a test that renders this template and check the desired output:

```
handlers/1_first_handlers/test/integration/rendering_test.rb
test ".merb template handler" do
  get "/handlers/merb"
  expected = "<p>MERB template handler is <strong>cool and fast</strong>!</p>"
  assert_match expected, response.body.strip
end
```

This time, to implement our template handler we won't use a lambda. Instead, let's create a module that responds to call(), allowing us to break our implementation into smaller methods. To compile to ERB, we'll simply use the ERB handler that ships with Rails, which we can retrieve using the ActionView::Template.registered_template_handler() method, as we did in *Writing the Code*, on page 43. Here's our .merb template handler:

```
handlers/1_first_handlers/lib/handlers.rb
module Handlers
  module MERB
    def self.erb_handler
      @@erb_handler ||= ActionView::Template.registered_template_handler(:erb)
    end

    def self.call(template)
      compiled_source = erb_handler.call(template)
      "RDiscount.new(begin;#{compiled_source};end).to_html"
    end
  end
end
```

```
ActionView::Template.register_template_handler :merb, Handlers::MERB
```

The ERB handler compiles the template, and like any other template handler, it returns a string with valid Ruby code. The result this Ruby code returns is a String containing Markdown syntax that is then converted to HTML using RDiscount.

Finally, look at how we wrapped the code returned by ERB in an inline begin/end clause. We have to do this inline, or it will mess up backtrace lines. For instance, imagine the following template:

```
<% nil.this_method_does_not_exist! %>
```

This template will raise an error when rendered. However, consider those two ways to compile the template:

```
RDiscount.new(begin
  nil.this_method_does_not_exist!
end).to_html
```

```
RDiscount.new(begin;nil.this_method_does_not_exist!;end).to_html
```

In the first example, since we introduced new lines in the compiled template, the exception backtrace would say the error happened in the second line of the template, which would be misleading. Notice we also need to use begin/end to wrap the code; otherwise, our handler would generate invalid Ruby code when the template contains more than one Ruby expression. Let's verify this by trying the following sample code in irb:

```
puts(a=1;b=a+1)             # => raises syntax error
puts(begin;a=1;b=a+1;end) # => prints 2 properly
```

The last line in our implementation registers our new handler, making all tests pass. Our .merb template handler is already implemented, but it still does not render both plain-text and HTML templates as described at the beginning of this chapter—it renders only the latter. We need to make a couple of changes to our template handler to output different results depending on the template format.

Multipart Emails

We'll use multipart emails in Action Mailer to showcase the behavior we want to add to our template handler. Let's create a mailer inside our dummy application to be used by our tests:

```
handlers/2_final/test/dummy/app/mailers/notifier.rb
class Notifier < ActionMailer::Base
  def contact(recipient)
    @recipient = recipient

    mail(to: @recipient, from: "john.doe@example.com") do |format|
      format.text
      format.html
    end
  end
end
```

This code should look familiar; just like respond_to() in your controllers, you can give a block to mail() to specify which templates to render. However, in controllers Rails chooses only one template to render, whereas in mailers the block specifies several templates that are used to create a single multipart email.

Our email has two parts, one in plain text and another in HTML. Since both parts will use the same template, let's create a template inside our dummy app, but without adding a format to its filename:

```
handlers/2_final/test/dummy/app/views/notifier/contact.merb
Dual templates **rock**!
```

And let's write a test for that using this mailer and view:

handlers/2_final/test/integration/rendering_test.rb

```ruby
test "dual template with .merb" do
  email = Notifier.contact("you@example.com")
  assert_equal 2, email.parts.size
  assert_equal "multipart/alternative", email.mime_type

  assert_equal "text/plain", email.parts[0].mime_type
  assert_equal "Dual templates **rock**!",
    email.parts[0].body.encoded.strip

  assert_equal "text/html", email.parts[1].mime_type
  assert_equal "<p>Dual templates <strong>rock</strong>!</p>",
    email.parts[1].body.encoded.strip
end
```

The test asserts that our email has two parts. Since the plain-text part is an alternative representation of the HTML part, the email should have a MIME type equal to multipart/alternative, which is automatically set by Action Mailer. The test then proceeds by checking the MIME type and body of each part. The order of the parts is also important; if the parts were inverted, most clients would simply ignore the HTML part, showing only plain text.

When we run this test, it fails because our text/plain part contains HTML code, not only plain text. This is expected, since our template handler always returns HTML code. To make it pass, we'll need to slightly change the implementation of Handlers::MERB.call() to consider the template.formats:

handlers/2_final/lib/handlers.rb

```ruby
def self.call(template)
  compiled_source = erb_handler.call(template)
  if template.formats.include?(:html)
    "RDiscount.new(begin;#{compiled_source};end).to_html"
  else
    compiled_source
  end
end
```

We inspect template.formats and check whether it includes the :html format. If so, we render the template as HTML; otherwise, we return the code that ERB compiled, resulting in a plain-text template written in Markdown syntax. This allows us to send an email with both plain-text and HTML parts using just one template!

With this last change, our template handler does exactly what we planned at the beginning of this chapter. Before we create generators for our new template handler, let's discuss how template.formats is set.

Formats Lookup

In *Writing the Code*, on page 43, we discussed that the resolver is responsible for giving the :format option to templates. The resolver does the following lookup to decide which format to use:

1. If the template found has a valid format, it is used. In templates placed in the filesystem, the format is specified in the template filename, as in index.html.erb.

2. If the template found does not specify a format, the resolver asks the template handler whether it has a default format.

3. If the template handler has no preferred format, the resolver should return the same formats used in the lookup.

Because our contact.merb template doesn't specify a format, the resolver tries to retrieve the default format from our Handlers::MERB template handler. This default format is retrieved through Handlers::MERB.default_format(), but since our template handler does not respond to default_format(), the second step is also skipped. The resolver's last option is to return the formats used in the lookup. As we're using format.text and format.html methods, they automatically set the formats in the lookup to plain text and HTML, respectively.

For instance, if we defined Handlers::MERB.default_format() in our implementation to return :text or :html, our last test would fail. Our resolver would never reach the third step and would always return a specific format in the second step.

4.3 Customizing Rails Generators

With our template handler in hand and rendering multipart emails, the final step is to create a generator for our plug-in. Our generator will hook into Rails's mailer generator and configure it to create .merb instead of .erb templates.

Rails generators provide hooks to allow other generators to extend and customize the generated code. A quick look at the mailer generator in the Rails source code reveals the hooks it provides:

```
rails/railties/lib/rails/generators/rails/mailer/mailer_generator.rb
module Rails
  module Generators
    class MailerGenerator < NamedBase
      source_root File.expand_path("../templates", __FILE__)
      argument :actions, type: :array,
        default: [], banner: "method method"
      check_class_collision
      def create_mailer_file
        template "mailer.rb",
```

```
        File.join("app/mailers", class_path, "#{file_name}.rb")
      end
      hook_for :template_engine, :test_framework
    end
  end
end
```

Although we haven't covered the whole Generators API yet, we can see that its main behavior is to copy a mailer template to app/mailers, which is implemented in the create_mailer_file() method. Notice the mailer generator does not say anything about the template engine or the test framework; it provides only hooks. This allows other libraries, like Haml and RSpec, to hook into the mailer generator, customizing the generation process.

The Active Model API and the decoupling in Rails generators provide important abstractions that allow us to replace Rails's defaults with our own conventions. We discussed the former in Chapter 2, *Building Models with Active Model*, on page 17, and now we'll play with the latter.

A Generator's Structure

To see how a generator works, let's take a deeper look at the Rails::Generators::MailerGenerator shown in the code on page 71. The mailer generator inherits from Rails::Generators::NamedBase. All generators that inherit from it expect an argument called NAME to be given when the generator is invoked from the command line. We can verify the arguments and options the mailer generator expects by executing the following command inside a Rails application:

```
$ rails g mailer --help
Usage:
  rails generate mailer NAME [method method] [options]

Options:
  -e, [--template-engine=NAME]   # Template engine to be invoked
                                 # Default: erb
  -t, [--test-framework=NAME]    # Test framework to be invoked
                                 # Default: test_unit
```

Back to our generator code—the Rails::Generators::MailerGenerator class also defines :actions as an argument, on line 6. Since a default value was provided (an empty array), these actions are optional and appear between brackets in the preceding help message.

Next, we invoke the class_collisions_check() method, which verifies that the NAME given to the generator is not already defined in our application. This is useful since it raises an error if we try to define a mailer named, for instance, Object.

On the next lines, we define the create_mailer_file() method, reproduced here for convenience:

```
def create_mailer_file
  template "mailer.rb",
    File.join("app/mailers", class_path, "#{file_name}.rb")
end
```

Rails generators work by invoking all public methods in the sequence they are defined. This construction is interesting because it plays well with inheritance: if you have to extend the mailer generator to do some extra tasks, you just need to inherit from it and define more public methods. Skipping a task is a matter of undefining some method. Whenever your new generator is invoked, it will execute the inherited methods and then the new public methods you defined. As with Rails controllers, you can expose or run actions by accident by leaving a method declared as public.

The create_mailer_file() method invokes three methods: template(), class_path(), and file_name(). The first one is a helper defined in Thor,[3] which is the basis for Rails generators, and the others are defined by Rails::Generators::NamedBase.

Thor has a module called Thor::Actions, which contains several methods to assist in generating tasks. One of them is the previously discussed template() method, which accepts two arguments: a source file and a destination.

The template() method reads the source file in the filesystem, executes the embedded Ruby code in it using ERB, and then copies the result to the given destination. All ERB templates in Thor are evaluated in the generator context, which means that instance variables defined in your generator are also available in your templates, as well as in protected/private methods.

The values returned by the two other methods, class_path() and file_name(), are inflected from the NAME given as an argument. To see all the defined methods and what they return, let's peek at the named_base_test.rb file in the Rails source code:

rails/railties/test/generators/named_base_test.rb
```
def test_named_generator_attributes
  g = generator ['admin/foo']
  assert_name g, 'admin/foo',   :name
  assert_name g, %w(admin),     :class_path
  assert_name g, 'Admin::Foo',  :class_name
  assert_name g, 'admin/foo',   :file_path
  assert_name g, 'foo',         :file_name
  assert_name g, 'Foo',         :human_name
```

---

3.   https://github.com/wycats/thor

```
  assert_name g, 'foo',        :singular_name
  assert_name g, 'foos',       :plural_name
  assert_name g, 'admin.foo',  :i18n_scope
  assert_name g, 'admin_foos', :table_name
end
```

This test asserts that when admin/foo is given as NAME, as in rails g mailer admin/foo, we can access all those methods, and each of them will return the respective value given in the assertion.

Finally, the mailer generator provides two hooks: one for the template engine and another for the test framework. Those hooks become options that can be given through the command line, as well. Summing it all up, the previous generator accepts a range of arguments and options and could be invoked as follows:

```
$ rails g mailer Notifier welcome contact --test-framework=rspec
```

Generators' Hooks

We already know Rails generators provide hooks. However, when we ask to use ERB as the template engine, how does the mailer generator know how to find and use it? Generators' hooks work thanks to a set of conventions. When you pick a template engine named :erb, the Rails::Generators::MailerGenerator will try to load one of the following three generators:

- Rails::Generators::ErbGenerator
- Erb::Generators::MailerGenerator
- ErbGenerator

And since all generators should be in the $LOAD_PATH, under the rails/generators or the generators folder, finding these generators is as simple as trying to require the following files:

- (rails/)generators/rails/erb/erb_generator
- (rails/)generators/rails/erb_generator
- (rails/)generators/erb/mailer/mailer_generator
- (rails/)generators/erb/mailer_generator
- (rails/)generators/erb/erb_generator
- (rails/)generators/erb_generator

If one of those generators is found, it is invoked with the same command-line arguments given to the mailer generator. In this case, the generator found is Erb::Generators::MailerGenerator, which we'll discuss next.

Template-Engine Hooks

Rails exposes three hooks for template engines: one for the controller, one for the mailer, and one for the scaffold generators. The first two generate files only if some actions are supplied on the command line, such as in rails g mailer Notifier welcome contact or rails g controller Info about contact. For each action given, the template engine should create a template for it.

On the other hand, the scaffold hook creates all views used in the scaffold: index, edit, show, new, and the _form partial.

The implementation of Erb::Generators::ControllerGenerator in Rails is as follows:

rails/railties/lib/rails/generators/erb/controller/controller_generator.rb
```
require "rails/generators/erb"
module Erb
  module Generators
    class ControllerGenerator < Base
      argument :actions, type: :array,
        default: [], banner: "action action"

      def copy_view_files
        base_path = File.join("app/views", class_path, file_name)
        empty_directory base_path
        actions.each do |action|
          @action = action
          @path = File.join(base_path, filename_with_extensions(action))
          template filename_with_extensions(:view), @path
        end
      end
    end
  end
end
```

The only method we haven't discussed yet is filename_with_extensions(), defined in Erb::Generators::Base:

rails/railties/lib/rails/generators/erb.rb
```
require "rails/generators/named_base"

module Erb
  module Generators
    class Base < Rails::Generators::NamedBase
      protected
      def format
        :html
      end
      def handler
        :erb
      end
```

```
    def filename_with_extensions(name)
      [name, format, handler].compact.join(".")
    end
  end
end
end
```

The Erb::Generators::ControllerGenerator creates a view file in app/views using the configured format and handler for each action given. The template used to create such views in the Rails source code looks like this:

rails/railties/lib/rails/generators/erb/controller/templates/view.html.erb
```
<h1><%= class_name %>#<%= @action %></h1>
<p>Find me in <%= @path %></p>
```

This, for rails g controller admin/foo bar, outputs the following in the file app/views/admin/foo/bar.html.erb:

```
<h1>Admin::Foo#bar</h1>
<p>Find me in app/views/admin/foo/bar</p>
```

The Erb::Generators::MailerGenerator class simply inherits from the previous controller generator and changes the default format to be :text, reusing the same logic:

rails/railties/lib/rails/generators/erb/mailer/mailer_generator.rb
```
require "rails/generators/erb/controller/controller_generator"

module Erb
  module Generators
    class MailerGenerator < ControllerGenerator
      protected

      def format
        :text
      end
    end
  end
end
```

And the template created for mailers looks like this:

rails/railties/lib/rails/generators/erb/mailer/templates/view.text.erb
```
<%= class_name %>#<%= @action %>

<%%= @greeting %>, find me in app/views/<%= @path %>
```

If we glance at the ERB generator's directory structure in the Rails source code at the railties/lib directory, we can easily see which templates are available, as in Figure 10, *Structure for ERB generators*, on page 77.

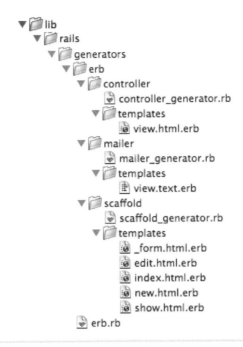

Figure 10—Structure for ERB generators

Therefore, if we want to completely replace ERB generators, we need to create those generators and templates. And since Rails generators play well with inheritance, we can do that by inheriting from the respective ERB generator and overwriting a few configuration methods.

Creating Our First Generator

All we need to do to implement our .merb mailer generator is inherit from Erb::Generators::MailerGenerator and overwrite both format() and handler() methods defined in Erb::Generators::Base. Our generator implementation looks like this:

handlers/2_final/lib/generators/merb/mailer/mailer_generator.rb
```ruby
require "rails/generators/erb/mailer/mailer_generator"

module Merb
  module Generators
    class MailerGenerator < Erb::Generators::MailerGenerator
      source_root File.expand_path("../templates", __FILE__)

      protected
      def format
        nil # Our templates have no format
      end
```

```ruby
      def handler
        :merb
      end
    end
  end
end
```

We need to invoke a method called source_root() at the class level to tell Rails the templates for our generator can be found at lib/generators/merb/mailer/templates.

Since we chose nil as the format and :merb as the handler, let's create our template view.merb with the following content:

handlers/2_final/lib/generators/merb/mailer/templates/view.merb
```
<%= class_name %>#<%= @action %>

<%%= @greeting %>, find me in app/views/<%= @path %>
```

And that's it. Our template has the same contents as in the ERB generator, but we could modify it to include some Markdown by default. To try the generator, let's move to the dummy application inside our plug-in at test/dummy and invoke the following command:

```
$ rails g mailer Mailer contact welcome --template-engine=merb
```

That command creates a mailer named Mailer with two templates, contact.merb and welcome.merb. The generator runs, showing us the following output:

```
create  app/mailers/mailer.rb
invoke  merb
create    app/views/mailer
create    app/views/mailer/contact.merb
create    app/views/mailer/welcome.merb
```

You can also configure your application at test/dummy/config/application.rb to use the merb generator by default, by adding the following line:

```
config.generators.mailer template_engine: :merb
```

However, you may not want to add this line to each new application you start. It would be nice if we could set this value as the default inside our plug-in and not always in the application. Rails allows us to do it with a Rails::Railtie.

4.4 Extending Rails with Railties

A Rails::Railtie (pronounced "Rails Rail-tie") allows you to hook into Rails's initialization and configure some defaults. Such tools allow frameworks like Active Record to tell Rails how it should be initialized and configured by providing a railtie.

You should include a railtie in your plug-in only if at least one of the following is true:

- Your plug-in needs to perform a given task while or after the Rails application is initialized.
- Your plug-in needs to change a configuration value—for instance, setting a generator.
- Your plug-in must provide Rake tasks and generators in nondefault locations (the default location for the former is lib/tasks, and it's lib/generators or lib/rails/generators for the latter).
- Your plug-in wants to run custom code whenever the Rails console or the Rails runner is started.
- You want your plug-in to provide configuration options to the application, such as config.my_plugin.key = :value.

Let's look at an excerpt of ActiveRecord::Railtie in the Rails source code that contains a few examples of these scenarios:

`rails/activerecord/lib/active_record/railtie.rb`
```ruby
module ActiveRecord
  class Railtie < Rails::Railtie
    config.active_record = ActiveSupport::OrderedOptions.new
    config.app_generators.orm :active_record, migration: true,
                                               timestamps: true
    config.app_middleware.insert_after "::ActionDispatch::Callbacks",
      "ActiveRecord::QueryCache"
    config.eager_load_namespaces << ActiveRecord
    rake_tasks do
      require "active_record/base"
      load "active_record/railties/databases.rake"
    end
    runner do
      require "active_record/base"
    end
    initializer "active_record.initialize_timezone" do
      ActiveSupport.on_load(:active_record) do
        self.time_zone_aware_attributes = true
        self.default_timezone = :utc
      end
    end
    initializer "active_record.migration_error" do
      if config.active_record.delete(:migration_error) == :page_load
        config.app_middleware.insert_after "::ActionDispatch::Callbacks",
          "ActiveRecord::Migration::CheckPending"
      end
    end
  end
end
```

After such examples, we are ready to create our first railtie and configure the mailer generator to use our new template handler by default:

handlers/2_final/lib/handlers/railtie.rb
```
module Handlers
  class Railtie < Rails::Railtie
    config.app_generators.mailer template_engine: :merb
  end
end
```

Since our railtie must be loaded when our plug-in is loaded, we need to add a require in lib/handlers.rb:

handlers/2_final/lib/handlers.rb
```
require "handlers/railtie"
```

And that's all! Let's go to the dummy application at test/dummy and invoke the generator helper once again with rails g mailer --help. Notice the default template engine has changed to *merb*. Therefore, we don't need to pass it as an option when invoking it!

All major Rails generators, such as model, controller, and scaffold, rely on hooks. As we've just seen, this allows us to adapt them to our workflow and preferred tools.

Importantly, this mechanism works only if our railtie is loaded before our application is initialized. This is why, in a freshly generated Rails application, we require our dependencies before we define the Rails application. You can verify that our dependencies are required early on by opening config/application.rb in any Rails application and observing that the Bundler.require line comes before we inherit from Rails::Application.

Furthermore, even though plug-ins are allowed to change Rails defaults, the application still has the final word about it. For instance, we changed Rails to use our :merb template engine in the mailer generator by default. However, if developers want to set this value back to :erb, they can simply do it inside the application definition at config/application.rb.

4.5 Wrapping Up

In this chapter, we finished our discussion about Rails's rendering stack by building a few template handlers. Our main template handler with the .merb extension mixes Markdown with ERB, allowing it to render both HTML and plain-text parts in an email by using just one template.

At the end of the chapter, we created a generator and customized Rails to use our new template handler by default. There is much more to discover in the

Generators API. Besides the methods seen in this chapter, Thor::Actions defines copy_file(), inject_into_file(), create_file(), run(), and a few more. In addition, Rails has a module called Rails::Generators::Actions that provides methods specific to Rails, such as gem(), environment(), route(), and many others. Rails also provides a testing facility to generators called Rails::Generators::TestCase, which is useful when testing our generators. Here is an example of how Rails uses Rails::Generators::TestCase to test its own mailer generator:

rails/railties/test/generators/mailer_generator_test.rb
```ruby
require "generators/generators_test_helper"
require "rails/generators/mailer/mailer_generator"

class MailerGeneratorTest < Rails::Generators::TestCase
  arguments %w(notifier foo bar)

  def test_mailer_skeleton_is_created
    run_generator
    assert_file "app/mailers/notifier.rb" do |mailer|
      assert_match(/class Notifier < ActionMailer::Base/, mailer)
      assert_match(/default from: "from@example.com"/, mailer)
    end
  end

  def test_mailer_with_i18n_helper
    run_generator
    assert_file "app/mailers/notifier.rb" do |mailer|
      assert_match(/en\.notifier\.foo\.subject/, mailer)
      assert_match(/en\.notifier\.bar\.subject/, mailer)
    end
  end

  def test_invokes_default_test_framework
    run_generator
    assert_file "test/mailers/notifier_test.rb" do |test|
      assert_match(/class NotifierTest < ActionMailer::TestCase/, test)
      assert_match(/test "foo"/, test)
      assert_match(/test "bar"/, test)
    end
  end
end
```

Be sure to explore all the tools available to you! Next we'll build a Rails engine that uses Rails's streaming functionalities to push updates to the browser as changes happen in our system.

In this chapter, we'll see
- Rails engines
- Rails live-streaming functionality
- Ruby threads and queues
- Eager loading of code in Rails

CHAPTER 5

Streaming Server Events to Clients Asynchronously

In the previous chapters, we analyzed the Rails rendering stack inside and out. You learned that when a request reaches a controller, the controller gathers the required information to render a template. The template is retrieved from one of the resolvers, compiled, rendered fully, and embedded in a layout. At the end of this process, you have a Ruby string representing this template. The string is set as the HTTP response and sent back to the client.

This approach works fine for the vast majority of applications. However, in some cases we need to send our response in smaller chunks. Sometimes, those smaller chunks may be infinite; we keep on sending chunks to the client until the connection between the server and the client is closed.

Whenever we send a response in chunks, we say the server is *streaming* data to the client. Since Rails was built with the more traditional request-response scenario in mind, streaming support was added and improved in Rails over time, and we'll explore it in this chapter.

To explore how streaming works, let's write a Rails plug-in that sends data to the browser whenever one of our style sheets changes. The browser will use this information to reload the current page style sheets, allowing developers to see changes in the HTML page as they modify their assets file, without a need to manually refresh the page in the web browser.

Since this plug-in is going to have its own controller, assets, routes, and more, we'll rely on the power provided by Rails engines so we can add those functionalities as if they were part of a Rails application, but then bundle it in a gem to share across different projects.

5.1 Extending Rails with Engines

Rails engines allow our plug-in to have its own controllers, models, helpers, views, assets, and routes, just like in a regular Rails application. Let's generate a plug-in called live_assets using the Rails plug-in generator. But this time we'll pass the --full flag, which will generate directories for models, controllers, routes, and more:

```
$ rails plug-in new live_assets --full
```

In addition to the files the generator normally creates for us, the --full flag also generates these files:

- An app directory with controllers, models, and others seen in a regular application

- A config/routes.rb file for routes

- A lib/live_assets/engine.rb file declaring our engine

- An empty test/integration/navigation_test.rb file to which we can add our integration tests

The most important file here is lib/live_assets/engine.rb, so let's take a closer look at it:

```
live_assets/1_live/lib/live_assets/engine.rb
module LiveAssets
  class Engine < ::Rails::Engine
  end
end
```

To create an engine, we need to inherit from Rails::Engine and ensure our new engine is loaded as soon as possible. The generator we ran already did this for us by placing this line in lib/live_assets.rb:

```
live_assets/1_live/lib/live_assets.rb
require "live_assets/engine"

module LiveAssets
end
```

Creating a Rails::Engine is quite similar to creating a Rails::Railtie. This is because a Rails::Engine is nothing more than a Rails::Railtie with some default initializers and the Paths application programming interface (API), which we'll see next.

Paths

A Rails::Engine does not have hard-coded paths. This means we are not required to place our models or controllers in app/; we can put them anywhere we choose. For instance, we can configure our engine to load our controllers from lib/controllers instead of app/controllers, as follows:

```ruby
module LiveAssets
  class Engine < Rails::Engine
    paths["app/controllers"] = ["lib/controllers"]
  end
end
```

We can also have Rails load our controllers from both app/controllers and lib/controllers:

```ruby
module LiveAssets
  class Engine < Rails::Engine
    paths["app/controllers"] << "lib/controllers"
  end
end
```

Those paths have the same semantics as in a Rails application: if you have a controller named LiveAssetsController inside app/controllers/live_assets_controller.rb or lib/controllers/live_assets_controller.rb, the controller will be loaded automatically when you need it. It doesn't need to be explicitly required.

For now, we'll follow the conventional path and stick our controllers in app/controllers, so don't apply the previous changes. We can check all customizable paths for an engine by inspecting the Rails source code:

rails/railties/lib/rails/engine/configuration.rb
```ruby
def paths
  @paths ||= begin
    paths = Rails::Paths::Root.new(@root)

    paths.add "app",                      eager_load: true, glob: "*"
    paths.add "app/assets",               glob: "*"
    paths.add "app/controllers",          eager_load: true
    paths.add "app/helpers",              eager_load: true
    paths.add "app/models",               eager_load: true
    paths.add "app/mailers",              eager_load: true
    paths.add "app/views"

    paths.add "app/controllers/concerns", eager_load: true
    paths.add "app/models/concerns",      eager_load: true

    paths.add "lib",                      load_path: true
    paths.add "lib/assets",               glob: "*"
    paths.add "lib/tasks",                glob: "**/*.rake"

    paths.add "config"
    paths.add "config/environments",      glob: "#{Rails.env}.rb"
    paths.add "config/initializers",      glob: "**/*.rb"
```

```
    paths.add "config/locales",      glob: "*.{rb,yml}"
    paths.add "config/routes.rb"

    paths.add "db"
    paths.add "db/migrate"
    paths.add "db/seeds.rb"

    paths.add "vendor",              load_path: true
    paths.add "vendor/assets",       glob: "*"

    paths
  end
end
```

The previous snippet shows that the engine also specifies which paths should be eager-loaded and which ones should not, plus it lists paths to locales, migrations, and more. However, declaring a path is not enough; something has to be done with the path. That's where initializers come in.

Initializers

An engine has several initializers that are responsible for booting the engine. These initializers are relatively low-level and should not be confused with the ones available inside your application's config/initializers. Let's explore an example:

rails/railties/lib/rails/engine.rb
```
initializer :add_view_paths do
  views = paths["app/views"].existent
  unless views.empty?
    ActiveSupport.on_load(:action_controller){ prepend_view_path(views) }
    ActiveSupport.on_load(:action_mailer){ prepend_view_path(views) }
  end
end
```

This initializer is responsible for adding our engine views, usually defined in app/views, to ActionController::Base and ActionMailer::Base as soon as they are loaded, allowing a Rails application to use the templates defined in an engine. To see all initializers defined in a Rails::Engine, we can start a new Rails console under test/dummy with rails console and type the following:

```
Rails::Engine.initializers.map(&:name) # =>
  [:set_load_path, :set_autoload_paths, :add_routing_paths,
   :add_locales, :add_view_paths, :load_environment_config,
   :append_assets_path, :prepend_helpers_path,
   :load_config_initializers, :engines_blank_point]
```

Working with an engine is pretty much the same as working with a Rails application. Since we know how to build applications, implementing our streaming plug-in should feel familiar.

5.2   Live Streaming

To see how streaming works, let's create a controller called LiveAssetsController at app/controllers/live_assets_controller.rb that includes the ActionController::Live functionality and streams "hello world" continuously:

```
live_assets/1_live/app/controllers/live_assets_controller.rb
class LiveAssetsController < ActionController::Base
  include ActionController::Live

  def hello
    while true
      response.stream.write "Hello World\n"
      sleep 1
    end
  rescue IOError
    response.stream.close
  end
end
```

Our controller provides an action named hello() that streams Hello World every second. If, for any reason, the connection between the server and the client drops, response.stream.write will fail with IOError, which we need to rescue before properly closing our stream.

We also need a route for the action hello():

```
live_assets/1_live/config/routes.rb
Rails.application.routes.draw do
  get "/live_assets/:action", to: "live_assets"
end
```

We are almost ready to try out our streaming endpoint. However, since a Rails engine cannot run on its own, we need to start it via the application in test/dummy. Furthermore, the streaming functionality doesn't work in WEBrick, the server that ships with Ruby and that Rails uses by default; WEBrick would buffer our response before sending it to the client and, given that our response is infinite, we would never see anything. For this reason, let's add Puma to our gemspec as a development dependency:[1]

```
live_assets/1_live/live_assets.gemspec
s.add_development_dependency "puma"
```

Finally, let's go into the test/dummy directory and run rails s. Rails now starts Puma instead of WEBrick:

---

1.   http://puma.io/

```
=> Booting Puma
=> Rails 4.0.0 application starting in development on http://0.0.0.0:3000
=> Call with -d to detach
=> Ctrl-C to shutdown server
```

Most browsers will also try to buffer the streaming response, and it may take a while before they decide to show us anything. So, to test that our streaming endpoint really works, we'll use cURL,[2] which works via the command line. Let's give curl a try:

```
$ curl -v localhost:3000/live_assets/hello
> GET /live_assets/hello HTTP/1.1
> User-Agent: curl/7.24.0 (x86_64-apple-darwin12.0)
> Host: localhost:3000
> Accept: */*
>
< HTTP/1.1 200 OK
< X-Frame-Options: SAMEORIGIN
< X-XSS-Protection: 1; mode=block
< X-Content-Type-Options: nosniff
< X-UA-Compatible: chrome=1
< Cache-Control: no-cache
< Content-Type: text/html; charset=utf-8
< X-Request-Id: f21f8c0d-d496-4bfa-944c-cd01b44b87ee
< X-Runtime: 0.003120
< Transfer-Encoding: chunked
<
Hello World
Hello World
```

Each second, you will see a new "Hello World" line appear on the screen. This means our streaming endpoint is working. Press CTRL+C on your keyboard to stop it, as we are ready to move on to more complex examples!

Server-Sent Events

Developers have always needed to receive updates from the server in the browser. For a long time, polling was the most common technique to solve this problem. In polling, the browser makes frequent requests to the server, asking for new data. In case no new information is available, the server returns an empty response and the browser starts a new request. Depending on the frequency, the browser ends up sending many requests to the server, generating a lot of overhead.

---

2.   http://curl.haxx.se/

Over time, techniques like *long polling* appeared. With it, the browser period-
ically sends requests the server, and if no updates are available the server
waits for some amount of time before sending an empty response. Although
it performs better than traditional polling, it's plagued with cross-compatibil-
ity issues between browsers. Furthermore, many proxies and servers drop a
connection if no communication happens for a while, making this approach
ineffective.

To address developers' update needs, the HTML5 specification includes two
new APIs: Server Sent Events (SSE) and WebSockets. WebSockets allows both
the client and server to exchange information over the same connection, but
since it is a new protocol, it may require changes in your deployment stack
to support it. On the other hand, Server Sent Events is a one-way communication channel from the server to the client, and can be used with any web
server that is able to stream responses. For those reasons, SSE is our tool of
choice for this chapter.

SSE's underpinning is the *event stream format*; here is a sample event stream
response for an HTTP request:

```
< HTTP/1.1 200 OK
< Content-Type: text/event-stream
<
< event: some_channel
< data: {"hello":"world"}
<
< event: other_channel
< data: {"another":"message"}
```

Messages are delimited by two new lines. Each message may have an event
and associated data. In this case, the data is a JavaScript Object Notation
(JSON) payload, but it could be any text. This is the format we need to return
from the server when streaming. Let's create a new action called sse in our
LiveAssetsController that streams a reloadCSS event every second:

live_assets/1_live/app/controllers/live_assets_controller.rb
```ruby
def sse
  response.headers["Cache-Control"] = "no-cache"
  response.headers["Content-Type"]  = "text/event-stream"

  while true
    response.stream.write "event: reloadCSS\ndata: {}\n\n"
    sleep 1
  end
rescue IOError
  response.stream.close
end
```

It is similar to our first action except now we need to set the proper response content type and disable any caching. With the server ready, let's implement the client side with JavaScript:

live_assets/1_live/app/assets/javascripts/live_assets/application.js
```javascript
window.onload = function() {
  // 1. Connect to our event-stream
  var source = new EventSource('/live_assets/sse');

  // 2. This callback will be triggered on every reloadCSS event
  source.addEventListener('reloadCSS', function(e) {

    // 3. Load all CSS entries
    var sheets  = document.querySelectorAll("[rel=stylesheet]");
    var forEach = Array.prototype.forEach;

    // 4. For each entry, clone it, add it to the
    //    document and remove the original after
    forEach.call(sheets, function(sheet){
      var clone = sheet.cloneNode();
      clone.addEventListener('load', function() {
        sheet.parentNode.removeChild(sheet);
      });
      document.head.appendChild(clone);
    });

  });
};
```

Our JavaScript file connects to our new endpoint and, on every reloadCSS event, it reloads all the style sheets on the page. Our assets file was defined at app/assets/live_assets/application.js; this structure is required because by default Rails precompiles only asset files matching application.*. Since they are the only files precompiled, such files usually include all other existing files in the project. That's why they are frequently called *manifests*.

Finally, let's create a helper that will make it easy for applications to load our assets:

live_assets/1_live/app/helpers/live_assets_helper.rb
```ruby
module LiveAssetsHelper
  def live_assets
    javascript_include_tag "live_assets/application"
  end
end
```

With our Server Sent Events mechanism ready, let's try it out. Go to our test/dummy application and create a controller and route:

live_assets/1_live/test/dummy/app/controllers/home_controller.rb
```ruby
class HomeController < ApplicationController
  def index
    render text: "Hello", layout: true
  end
end
```

live_assets/1_live/test/dummy/config/routes.rb
```ruby
Dummy::Application.routes.draw do
  root to: "home#index"
end
```

Change our layout to include the engine assets, but only in development:

live_assets/1_live/test/dummy/app/views/layouts/application.html.erb
```erb
<!DOCTYPE html>
<html>

<head>
  <title>Dummy</title>
  <%= stylesheet_link_tag "application", media: "all" %>
  <%= javascript_include_tag "application" %>
  <%= live_assets if Rails.env.development? %>
  <%= csrf_meta_tags %>
</head>

<body>
<%= yield %>
</body>

</html>
```

Restart the dummy app and point the browser to *localhost:3000*. If your browser has a network panel that shows all HTTP requests sent by the browser, you might expect each style sheet to be reloaded every second, but that's not what happens, as shown in Figure 11, *Pending application.css request on Google Chrome's network panel*, on page 92.

Even though Puma is a threaded web server, Rails allows only one thread to run at a time. Let's work around this issue by changing the dummy application to allow concurrency:

live_assets/1_live/test/dummy/config/application.rb
```ruby
config.allow_concurrency = true
```

Since the browser is connected to the web server, waiting for the server to accept requests, we need to close the browser before restarting the web server. Close the browser, restart the server, then reopen *localhost:3000*; we can finally see the stylesheet files reloading every second. To verify that our style

Name Path	Method	Status Text	Type
localhost	GET	200 OK	text/html
application.css?body=1 /assets	GET	304 Not Modified	text/css
application.js?body=1 /assets/live_assets	GET	304 Not Modified	application/javascript
application.js?body=1 /assets	GET	304 Not Modified	application/javascript
sse /live_assets	GET	200 OK	text/event-stream
application.css?body=1 /assets	GET	(pending)	Pending

Figure 11—Pending **application.css** request on Google Chrome's network panel

sheets reload, we can edit test/dummy/app/assets/stylesheets/application.css and observe that the changes happen live, without refreshing the page. For example, try setting the text color to red:

```
body { color: red; }
```

As you can see, our streaming of server-sent events works! However, we can make a few improvements. First, we want to reload the style sheets only when changes happen in the filesystem—not every second. Watching for those changes should be efficient. If we have five pages open, we don't want to query our filesystem for each open page; ideally, we'd have one main filesystem listener entity that each request can subscribe to.

The second problem in our code so far is that we haven't written any tests. This feature is particularly hard to test because we're streaming an infinite amount of data, so instead of testing it directly from the controller, we need to break all the existing components into smaller, testable chunks.

Finally, since we've enabled config.allow_concurrency, we need to understand how such a configuration will affect the deployment of applications that rely on streaming. So don't go anywhere yet: we still have a lot to do!

5.3 Filesystem Notifications with Threads

A Rails application is generated with three assets directories by default: app/assets, lib/assets, and vendor/assets. Our assets should be split between those directories in the same way we'd split our code: the app directory should contain assets related directly to our application, the lib directory should hold isolated JavaScript or stylesheet components that would be useful beyond our application, and the vendor directory should contain third-party files.

We'd like to watch for filesystem changes in each of these directories. One option is to manually check the modification time of each file in those directories every second or less. This is *filesystem polling*. Polling may be a good starting point, but as the number of assets grows, it can become very CPU intensive.

Luckily, most operating systems provide a notification mechanism for filesystem changes. We simply pass to the operating system all the directories we want to watch and, if a file is added, removed, or changed, our code will be notified. The *listen gem* exposes all major operating-system notifications mechanisms under a single, easy-to-use API.[3]

Also, given our requirement of having one main entity watching the filesystem that our requests can subscribe to, let's wrap all the listening functionality inside a thread, which will run alongside our requests concurrently. Let's open lib/live_assets.rb and implement it:

```
live_assets/2_listener/lib/live_assets.rb
require "live_assets/engine"
require "thread"
require "listen"
module LiveAssets
  mattr_reader :subscribers
  @@subscribers = []
  # Subscribe to all published events.
  def self.subscribe(subscriber)
    subscribers << subscriber
  end
  # Unsubscribe an existing subscriber.
  def self.unsubscribe(subscriber)
    subscribers.delete(subscriber)
  end
  # Start a listener for the following directories.
  # Every time a change happens, publish the given
  # event to all subscribers available.
  def self.start_listener(event, directories)
    Thread.new do
      Listen.to(*directories, latency: 0.5) do |_modified, _added, _removed|
        subscribers.each { |s| s << event }
      end
    end
  end
end
```

---

3. https://github.com/guard/listen

Our code provides a mechanism for starting listeners inside a thread. These listeners watch a given set of directories and, every time a change happens, they push the registered event to each of the subscribers. Since we're using the listen gem, let's add it to the gemspec, too:

live_assets/2_listener/live_assets.gemspec
```
s.add_dependency "listen"
```

Although we can't write integration tests for an action that streams filesystem updates infinitely, our listener functionality is decoupled from the streaming system, allowing us to test it in isolation. Let's write a test that starts a listener and verifies that an event will be pushed to our subscriber whenever a change happens in the test/tmp directory:

live_assets/2_listener/test/live_assets_test.rb
```
require "test_helper"
require "fileutils"

class LiveAssetsTest < ActiveSupport::TestCase
  setup do
    FileUtils.mkdir_p "test/tmp"
  end

  teardown do
    FileUtils.rm_rf "test/tmp"
  end

  test "can subscribe to listener events" do
    # Create a listener
    l = LiveAssets.start_listener(:reload, ["test/tmp"])
    # Our subscriber is a simple array
    subscriber = []
    LiveAssets.subscribe(subscriber)

    begin
      while subscriber.empty?
        # Trigger changes in a file until we get an event
        File.write("test/tmp/sample", SecureRandom.hex(20))
      end

      # Assert we got the event
      assert_includes subscriber, :reload
    ensure
      # Clean up
      LiveAssets.unsubscribe(subscriber)
      l.kill
    end
  end
end
```

Excellent! It seems our listener works as expected. As you run the test suite, you may get some warnings from the listen gem. This is because it uses filesystem polling unless you install a gem specific to your operating system that uses the filesystem notifications. Feel free to add such a gem to your Gemfile (and not to the gemspec, since it is not a strict dependency of our plug-in).

Finally, we need to ensure a listener that watches over the assets directories starts whenever our application boots, and pushes a :reloadCSS whenever there is a change. Let's write a test:

`live_assets/2_listener/test/live_assets_test.rb`
```ruby
test "can subscribe to existing reloadCSS events" do
  subscriber = []
  LiveAssets.subscribe(subscriber)

  begin
    while subscriber.empty?
      FileUtils.touch("test/dummy/app/assets/stylesheets/application.css")
    end

    assert_includes subscriber, :reloadCSS
  ensure
    LiveAssets.unsubscribe(subscriber)
  end
end
```

Our test assumes the listener is already available by the time the test runs. To make the test pass, let's define an initializer inside our engine, similar to the ones we saw earlier in this chapter, that starts the listener, passing all the asset directories as arguments:

`live_assets/2_listener/lib/live_assets/engine.rb`
```ruby
module LiveAssets
  class Engine < ::Rails::Engine
    initializer "live_assets.start_listener" do |app|
      paths = app.paths["app/assets"].existent +
              app.paths["lib/assets"].existent +
              app.paths["vendor/assets"].existent

      paths = paths.select { |p| p =~ /stylesheets/ }

      if app.config.assets.compile
        LiveAssets.start_listener :reloadCSS, paths
      end
    end
  end
end
```

Notice we start the listener only if our assets are being dynamically compiled; this avoids starting the listener in production, where assets are usually pre-compiled and the compile configuration is set to false.

Now that our listener is started by default and is ready to push events to subscribers, every time a new request is made of /*live_assets*/*sse*, we need to create a new subscriber, add it to the subscribers list, and *wait* until a new event is pushed to our subscriber. Once the event arrives, we stream a server-sent event to the browser, as the following figure shows.

Operating-System Notifications

```
┌────────────┐   ┌────────────┐   ┌─────────────┐
│ app/assets │   │ lib/assets │   │ vendor/assets│
└────────────┘   └────────────┘   └─────────────┘
```

LiveAssets

Subscriber   Subscriber

```
┌─────────────────┐  ┌─────────────────┐  ┌─────────────────┐
│ live_assets#sse │  │ live_assets#sse │  │ live_assets#sse │
└─────────────────┘  └─────────────────┘  └─────────────────┘

    SSE                  SSE                  SSE

┌──────────┐         ┌──────────┐         ┌──────────┐
│ Browser  │         │ Browser  │         │ Browser  │
└──────────┘         └──────────┘         └──────────┘
```

Figure 12—Visualization of the filesystem notifications stack

The tricky part in this schema is waiting: we want each request to be idle until an event arrives. Checking for a new event in a loop, as we did in the test, is not an option since it will cause the CPU to spike. We could work around this by sleeping for a specific amount of time, like half second, and then checking for an event, but this is also suboptimal. Ideally, we want to sleep for whatever time is necessary and automatically wake up as soon as an event arrives.

Ruby ships with a perfect solution in its Standard Library: the Queue class. Let's take a look at it.

Threads and Queues

A queue is a first-in, first-out data structure. We can make a queue implementation accessible to any Ruby code by requiring thread, and it provides a very simple API:

```ruby
require "thread"
q = Queue.new

t = Thread.new do
  while last = q.pop
    sleep(1) # simulate cost
    puts last
  end
end

q << :foo
sleep(1)
$stdout.flush
```

This code creates a new Queue and a new Thread. Inside the thread is a loop that calls Queue#pop(). If there is no item in the queue, the thread will block until an item is pushed to the queue. In the last three lines, we push a symbol to the queue, which will wake up the thread. After one second, if we flush what was written to $stdout, we'll see "foo" printed.

This means queues are the perfect structure for us to use as subscribers! If the queue is empty, the request is going to sleep until a new event arrives; then we stream this new event and go back to sleep. Let's create a class named LiveAssets::SSESubscriber that will receive those events and output them in the server-sent event stream format, as in the following test:

```ruby
live_assets/2_listener/test/live_assets/subscriber_test.rb
require "test_helper"
require "thread"
class LiveAssets::SubscriberTest < ActiveSupport::TestCase
  test "yields server sent events from the queue" do
    # Let's start our queue with some events
    queue = Queue.new
    queue << :reloadCSS
    queue << :ping
    queue << nil

    # And create a subscriber on top of it
    subscriber = LiveAssets::SSESubscriber.new(queue)
    stream = []
    subscriber.each do |msg|
      stream << msg
    end
```

```
      assert_equal 2, stream.length
      assert_includes stream, "event: reloadCSS\ndata: {}\n\n"
      assert_includes stream, "event: ping\ndata: {}\n\n"
    end
end
```

Our test creates a queue, passes it to a subscriber, and then consumes all events emitted by the subscriber. Notice we push nil to the queue as a way to signal we have no more events to consume. Let's implement the subscriber:

live_assets/2_listener/lib/live_assets/sse_subscriber.rb
```
require "thread"
module LiveAssets
  class SSESubscriber
    def initialize(queue = Queue.new)
      @queue = queue
      LiveAssets.subscribe(@queue)
    end

    def each
      while event = @queue.pop
        yield "event: #{event}\ndata: {}\n\n"
      end
    end

    def close
      LiveAssets.unsubscribe(@queue)
    end
  end
end
```

and autoload it:

live_assets/2_listener/lib/live_assets.rb
```
module LiveAssets
  autoload :SSESubscriber, "live_assets/sse_subscriber"
end
```

Finally, let's rewrite our live_assets#sse action to make use of our new subscriber:

live_assets/2_listener/app/controllers/live_assets_controller.rb
```
def sse
  response.headers["Cache-Control"] = "no-cache"
  response.headers["Content-Type"]  = "text/event-stream"

  sse = LiveAssets::SSESubscriber.new
  sse.each { |msg| response.stream.write msg }
rescue IOError
  sse.close
  response.stream.close
end
```

Once again, restart the Puma server running inside test/dummy and verify that event streams come only after you edit app/assets/stylesheets/application.css, reflecting immediate changes on the page. This time, let's make the font bigger:

```
body { font-size: 32px; }
```

We are almost done with our implementation; there's one last problem we have to tackle. In case no changes happen in a style sheet for some time, we can remain for a long period without streaming any data to the browser. This may cause the browser, the server, or even a proxy in between to close the connection.

Timer

To ensure the connection won't be closed due to long idle periods, we need a timer whose sole responsibility is to push a ping event to subscribers every ten seconds. Let's start by writing a test:

`live_assets/3_final/test/live_assets_test.rb`
```
test "receives timer notifications" do
  # Create a timer
  l = LiveAssets.start_timer(:ping, 0.5)

  # Our subscriber is a simple array
  subscriber = []
  LiveAssets.subscribe(subscriber)

  begin
    # Wait until we get an event
    true while subscriber.empty?
    assert_includes subscriber, :ping
  ensure
    # Clean up
    LiveAssets.unsubscribe(subscriber)
  end
end
```

Our timer will also run on its own thread and push events to the subscribers synchronously:

`live_assets/3_final/lib/live_assets.rb`
```
def self.start_timer(event, time)
  Thread.new do
    while true
      subscribers.each { |s| s << event }
      sleep(time)
    end
  end
end
```

This implementation is enough to make our test pass! Finally, let's add to our engine another initializer responsible for starting the timer:

```
live_assets/3_final/lib/live_assets/engine.rb
initializer "live_assets.start_timer" do |app|
  if app.config.assets.compile
    LiveAssets.start_timer :ping, 10
  end
end
```

Restart the Puma web server; now ping events should be sent every ten seconds. We have not registered any callback for such events on the JavaScript side, but we could if we desired. The JavaScript EventSource object also emits open and close events for when the connection is opened and closed. Mozilla's Developer Network has more information on server-sent events that you can explore.[4]

Throughout our implementation, one of the details we just glanced over was the need for setting config.allow_concurrency to true. Now, with the live-assets implementation out of the way, we have the perfect opportunity to discuss it.

5.4 Code-Loading Techniques

To understand why we need to explicitly turn on allow_concurrency, we need to analyze the mechanisms available in Ruby and Rails to load code.

The most common form of loading code is Ruby's require() method:

```
require "live_assets"
```

Some libraries work fine by simply using require, but as they grow, some of them tend to rely on autoload techniques to avoid loading all their files up front. Autoload is particularly important in Rails plug-ins because it helps application boot time to stay low in development and test environments, since we load modules only when we first need them.

Autoload techniques

We've used *Ruby's autoload* in this chapter with the LiveAssets::SSESubscriber class:

```
module LiveAssets
  autoload :SSESubscriber, "live_assets/sse_subscriber"
end
```

---

4.   https://developer.mozilla.org/en-US/docs/Server-sent_events/Using_server-sent_events

Now the first time LiveAssets::SSESubscriber is accessed, it will be automatically loaded. Rails plug-ins and applications have another code-loading technique, which is *Rails's autoload*. For example, our LiveAssetsController is automatically loaded when we first need it. But this case is not handled by Ruby, but rather by ActiveSupport::Dependencies, which ships with Rails.

The issue with both the Ruby and Rails approaches is that loading code in Ruby is not atomic—it does not occur in a single step. For example, if you have a request happening inside Thread A and that thread starts loading LiveAssetsController, the LiveAssetsController class can be visible from Thread B in another request *before* Thread A has finished loading the app/controllers/live_assets_controller.rb file. In this scenario, Thread B has a partial implementation of the controller, which, for example, could contain only the hello() action (and not the sse() one), leading to a failure.

Although some Ruby implementations have been working toward making Ruby's autoload thread-safe (so the scenario previously described won't happen), Rails's autoload is not thread-safe. To work around this fact, whenever Rails needs to autoload code, Rails allows only one thread to run by default, which means it can serve only one request at a time. That's why we could not serve assets at the same time the server-sent events connection was open. To work around this limitation, we have set config.allow_concurrency to true at our own risk.

What does this mean for production? Do we need to allow concurrency explicitly in production? What are our options to deploy this application?

Eager-Load Techniques

In production, Rails *eager-loads* your code: all of your models, controllers, helpers, and more are loaded on boot. Since all Rails code is loaded up front and there is no code reloading, autoloading is disabled. And when there is no autoload, we are safe to run our Rails application with config.allow_concurrency set to true, which Rails does for us by default.

However, Rails is only going to eager-load the code defined inside the app directory. If we're relying on Ruby autoload, we need to eager-load the code ourselves! Otherwise, we're possibly autoloading code in the middle of a request. This is what could happen with LiveAssets::SSESubscriber. Imagine this scenario:

On the first request to */live_assets/sse*, Ruby will start to load LiveAssets::SSESubscriber. If many requests happen to this endpoint at the same time, the first request may not have finished loading the subscriber, leading the following requests to see a partial definition of the subscriber. The solution is to ensure LiveAssets::SSESubscriber is eager-loaded when the Rails application boots. Since this is a common need in Rails plug-ins and in the Rails codebase itself, Rails provides some conveniences for us.

The first convenience is the config.eager_load_namespaces configuration option, available in any railtie or engine, that keeps a list of namespaces to eager-load. Let's add LiveAssets to this list in our engine definition:

```
live_assets/3_final/lib/live_assets/engine.rb
config.eager_load_namespaces << LiveAssets
```

Now Rails will call LiveAssets.eager_load! to explicitly eager-load our code on production. However, we haven't implemented the eager_load!() yet. Let's define it with the help of ActiveSupport::Autoload:

```
live_assets/3_final/lib/live_assets.rb
module LiveAssets
  extend ActiveSupport::Autoload

  eager_autoload do
    autoload :SSESubscriber
  end
end
```

By extending our module with ActiveSupport::Autoload, we automatically get a LiveAssets.eager_load! method that eager-loads everything defined inside the eager_autoload() block. We no longer need to pass a path to autoload(); Rails does its best to guess it based on the constant name.

That's all we need to do for Rails to eager-load the rest of our code. Remember—we'll use this technique every time we have code that Rails doesn't load automatically, usually set up via Ruby autoloads. We can open a console in the test/dummy directory to check all namespaces that Rails eager-loads:

```
Rails.application.config.eager_load_namespaces # =>
  [ ActiveSupport, ActionDispatch, ActiveModel, ActionView,
    ActionController, ActiveRecord, ActionMailer, LiveAssets::Engine,
    LiveAssets, Dummy::Application ]
```

Keep in mind that eager loading is not only beneficial for threaded web servers like Puma, but also for fork-based servers like Unicorn.[5] Unicorn operates by taking a snapshot of our Rails application just after it boots. By eager-loading our code, we guarantee that this snapshot contains all of our code loaded up front and we don't need to spend time autoloading the code on every request.

---

5. http://unicorn.bogomips.org/

Therefore, the decision of which web server to use when streaming is involved (and for long-lived requests it usually boils down to your web server's ability to handle many concurrent connections. For example, Unicorn works by starting a pool of web-server processes, and each web server is able to handle only one request at a time (the single-threaded multiprocess model). If one web server is streaming data or receiving a huge uploaded file, it is unable to serve other requests, even if data is streamed though the connection only every ten seconds! On the other hand, the Puma web server we used in this chapter is able to handle other requests even while we're streaming.

Unfortunately, there's no silver bullet, and the best option when it comes to deployment is to benchmark the different web servers available. Multithreaded web servers like Puma can handle multiple requests, as can evented servers like Thin; however, as of version 1.5, Thin still does not support streaming.[6] Servers like Passenger and Rainbows! allow you to mix different concurrency styles, so you have a hybrid multithreaded multiprocess deployment option.[7,8] To add more options to the mix, you may even get better results by deploying on platforms like JRuby and Rubinius.[9,10]

Different platforms offer developers different thread-safety guarantees. For instance, array operations in JRuby are not guaranteed to be safe, which is an issue in our plug-in. The LiveAssets.subscribers array is a global data structure, and it could happen that two requests try to subscribe at the exactly same time, corrupting our array. That said, we need to wrap our subscriber operations in a mutex, a structure that guarantees just one thread can execute a particular piece of code at a given moment:

live_assets/3_final/lib/live_assets.rb
```
@@mutex = Mutex.new
def self.subscribe(subscriber)
  @@mutex.synchronize do
    subscribers << subscriber
  end
end
def self.unsubscribe(subscriber)
  @@mutex.synchronize do
    subscribers.delete(subscriber)
  end
end
```

---

6. http://code.macournoyer.com/thin/
7. https://www.phusionpassenger.com/
8. http://rainbows.rubyforge.org
9. http://jruby.org/
10. http://rubini.us/

By running the tests again, our test suite should remain green and our code is now also thread-safe on JRuby! This is important to keep in mind: every time global state is manipulated in the middle of a request, we need to check which thread-safety guarantee each Ruby implementation gives us, and act accordingly. Only by writing thread-safe code we can rely on a variety of available deployment options.

5.5 Wrapping Up

In this chapter, we used Rails live-streaming functionalities to push server-sent events to the browser. Our implementation had a central entity listening for filesystem changes, which were pushed to a group of subscribers. We used Ruby's built-in threads and queues to control the information flow throughout our system.

The topics discussed in this chapter are a basis to introduce code-loading techniques in Rails, and how those techniques affect the deployment of our applications. We glanced over thread safety and the subtleties involved with different web servers and Ruby implementations.

Next let's see how to encapsulate our controllers' behavior in an object called ActionController::Responder and customize it to suit our needs! Then we'll discuss Rails generators and learn other ways to customize them.

In this chapter, we'll see
- Rails responders and the respond_with() method
- Rails generators' template customization

CHAPTER 6

Writing DRY Controllers with Responders

Rails's scaffold generator is a great tool to help us prototype a new application. Its flexibility lets us swap the default template engine, test framework, and object-relational mapper (ORM) for our favorite options, ensuring we are productive regardless of the tools we choose. The only problem with scaffolding is that the generated controllers are still a little bit verbose, and we end up with a lot of behavior duplicated across different controllers. For example, here are the create() and destroy() actions similar to what would be generated by the scaffold generator when invoked with a name attribute:

```ruby
class UsersController < ApplicationController
  def create
    @user = User.new(user_params)
    respond_to do |format|
      if @user.save
        format.html { redirect_to @user, notice: 'User was successfully created.' }
        format.json { render action: 'show', status: :created, location: @user }
      else
        format.html { render action: 'new' }
        format.json { render json: @user.errors, status: :unprocessable_entity }
      end
    end
  end

  def destroy
    @user = User.find(params[:id])
    @user.destroy
    respond_to do |format|
      format.html { redirect_to users_url }
      format.json { head :no_content }
    end
  end

  private
```

```
  def user_params
    params.require(:user).permit(:name)
  end
end
```

All of these respond_to() blocks are very similar from one controller to another. To solve this issue, Rails provides a method called respond_with(), which uses an ActionController::Responder to abstract how our controllers respond. Using this new application programming interface (API), these actions are reduced to the following:

```
class UsersController < ApplicationController
  respond_to :html, :json

  def create
    @user = User.new(user_params)
    flash[:notice] = 'User was successfully created.' if @user.save
    respond_with(@user)
  end

  def destroy
    @user = User.find(params[:id])
    @user.destroy
    respond_with(@user)
  end

  private

  def user_params
    params.require(:user).permit(:name)
  end
end
```

At the top we declare which formats our controller responds to, and delegate all the hard work to respond_with(). We could rewrite all of our actions using this cleaner API.

In this chapter, we'll cover how responders work, customize them to handle HTTP caching and flash messages automatically, and finally customize the scaffold generator to use respond_with() by default.

6.1   Understanding Responders

To understand the concepts behind responders, we must understand the three variables that affect how controllers respond: request type, HTTP verb, and resource status.

Navigational and API Requests

A controller the scaffold generator creates responds to two formats by default: HTML and JavaScript Object Notation (JSON). The scaffold generator uses these two formats because they represent two types of requests: navigational and API. The former is handled by a browser and holds formats like HTML and MOBILE, whereas the latter is used by machines and represents formats like XML and JSON.

```ruby
def index
  @users = User.all
  respond_to do |format|
    format.html # index.html.erb
    format.json { render json: @users }
  end
end
```

Let's analyze this index() action, common to many Rails applications. The HTML format receives no block, so it renders a template, and the JSON format renders the JSON representation of the resource with render json: @users.

This means the controllers' behavior depends on the request type. Consequently, to abstract how controllers work, responders should take the request type into account.

HTTP Verb

The show() and new() actions in a Rails controller respond similarly to index(), by rendering a template or a representation of the requested object. And what do all these actions have in common? The HTTP verb.

The remaining actions, such as create() and destroy(), are triggered by the POST and DELETE verbs, respectively, and they respond in a different fashion, redirecting to distinct places, returning distinct status codes and HTTP headers. In other words, the HTTP verb is another variable that affects how a controller responds.

Given the number of possible outcomes from a request, let's look closely at the scaffold controller Rails generates, and create a table representing how it responds depending on the request type and HTTP verb.

By default all GET requests, usually handled by actions like index(), show(), and new(), render a template for navigational requests. If we have an API request, we may either render a template (like a .jbuilder template) or render the resource representation (for example, by calling to_json() on it). Table 1, *Scaffold Resource Behavior for GET*, on page 108 summarizes this information.

	Navigational Request	API Request
GET	render template	render template or render resource.to_format
POST		
PUT		
DELETE		

Table 1—Scaffold Resource Behavior for GET

So far we know how a scaffolded controller responds to GET in both request types. Now let's run through the other HTTP verbs and fill in the whole table.

Resource Status

If we analyze the create() action, which represents a POST request, we realize that it has two branches: one if the resource is saved successfully, and the other if not. Each of these branches responds in a different way:

```
def create
  @user = User.new(user_params)

  respond_to do |format|
    if @user.save
      format.html { redirect_to @user, notice: 'User was successfully created.' }
      format.json { render action: 'show', status: :created, location: @user }
    else
      format.html { render action: "new" }
      format.json { render json: @user.errors, status: :unprocessable_entity }
    end
  end
end
```

The status of the resource determines how the scaffolded controller responds. In this case, we redirect if the resource is successfully created, but render a page with errors if creation fails. We can also see this pattern in the update() action, which is invoked by PATCH and PUT requests.

Although the destroy() action the scaffolding generates does not seem to depend on the resource status, we may eventually need to change the destroy() action to handle cases where resource.destroy returns false. For example, imagine a setup where a group has several managers. Because a group needs to have at least one manager, we implement a before_destroy() callback that checks for this condition every time we try to remove a manager. If the condition isn't met, both the callback and the destroy() method return false. This new scenario needs to be handled in the controller, usually by changing the destroy() action to show a flash message and redirect to the group page. In other words, even though the destroy() action the scaffold generates does not depend on the resource status, DELETE requests may.

That said, the controller needs to know the resource status in order to respond to POST, PUT, and DELETE requests. Our table is modified to represent this new scenario and filled in accordingly for each request type, HTTP verb, and resource status:

		Navigational	API
GET		render template	render template or resource.to_format
POST	Success	redirect_to resource	render template or resource.to_format
POST	Failure	render :new	render resource.errors
PUT	Success	redirect_to resource	head :no_content
PUT	Failure	render :edit	render resource.errors
DELETE	Success	redirect_to collection	head :no_content
DELETE	Failure	redirect_to collection	render resource.errors

Table 2—Scaffold Resource Behavior

Whenever you invoke respond_with() in your controllers, it calls the ActionController::Responder class, which is nothing more than this whole table written in Ruby code. Let's explore how ActionController::Responder is implemented and how we can modify it to behave in a custom way.

6.2 Exploring ActionController::Responder

Anything that responds to call(), accepting three arguments, can be a responder. The three arguments given to call() are the current controller, the resource (or a nested resource or an array of resources), and a hash of options. All the options given to respond_with() are forwarded to the responder as the third argument.

ActionController::Responder implements the call() method in a single line of code, as we can see in the Rails source code:

```
rails/actionpack/lib/action_controller/metal/responder.rb
def self.call(*args)
  new(*args).respond
end
```

The call() method forwards these three arguments to the ActionController::Responder initialization and then calls respond():

```
rails/actionpack/lib/action_controller/metal/responder.rb
# Main entry point for responder responsible
# for dispatching to the proper format.
def respond
  method = "to_#{format}"
  respond_to?(method) ? send(method) : to_format
end


# HTML format does not render the resource,
# it always attempts to render a template.
def to_html
  default_render
rescue ActionView::MissingTemplate => e
  navigation_behavior(e)
end


# to_js simply tries to render a template.
# If no template is found, raises the error.
def to_js
  default_render
end


# All other formats follow the procedure below. First we
# try to render a template. If the template is not available,
# we verify if the resource responds to :to_format and display it.
def to_format
  if get? || !has_errors? || response_overridden?
    default_render
  else
    display_errors
  end
rescue ActionView::MissingTemplate => e
  api_behavior(e)
end
```

The respond() method checks whether the responder handles the current request format. If so, it calls the specific method for this format; otherwise, it calls to_format(). Since ActionController::Responder defines only to_html() and to_js(), only HTML and JavaScript (JS) requests have a custom behavior, and all others fall back to the to_format() case.

By analyzing both to_html() and to_format() implementations, we see that the former responds with navigational_behavior() and the latter responds with api_behavior(). If we add a new navigational format to an application, such as MOBILE, the responder will treat it as an API format, not a navigational one. Luckily, because of how responders work, we can make MOBILE requests use the navigational behavior by simply aliasing the :to_mobile method to :to_html in an initializer.

```
ActionController::Responder.class_eval do
  alias :to_iphone :to_html
end
```

Additionally, note that a responder always invokes the default_render() method before falling back to the API or navigational behavior:

rails/actionpack/lib/action_controller/metal/responder.rb
```
def to_html
  default_render
rescue ActionView::MissingTemplate => e
  navigation_behavior(e)
end
```

default_render() simply tries to render a template in case none was rendered yet (performed?() must return false), and in case the template is not found, it raises an ActionView::MissingTemplate, which is properly rescued, allowing responders behavior to kick in.

Here's how Rails implements the navigational_behavior() and api_behavior() methods:

rails/actionpack/lib/action_controller/metal/responder.rb
```
DEFAULT_ACTIONS_FOR_VERBS = {
  post: :new,
  patch: :edit,
  put: :edit
}
# This is the common behavior for formats associated
# with browsing, like :html, :iphone and so forth.
def navigation_behavior(error)
  if get?
    raise error
  elsif has_errors? && default_action
    render :action => default_action
  else
    redirect_to navigation_location
  end
end

# This is the common behavior for formats associated
# with APIs, such as :xml and :json.
def api_behavior(error)
  raise error unless resourceful?
  if get?
    display resource
  elsif post?
    display resource, :status => :created, :location => api_location
  else
    head :no_content
  end
end
```

```ruby
def resourceful?
  resource.respond_to?("to_#{format}")
end

def has_errors?
  resource.respond_to?(:errors) && !resource.errors.empty?
end

def resource_location
  options[:location] || resources
end
alias :navigation_location :resource_location
alias :api_location :resource_location

# Display is just a shortcut to render a resource with the current format.
#
#   display @user, status: :ok
#
# For XML requests it's equivalent to:
#
#   render xml: @user, status: :ok
#
# Options sent by the user are also used:
#
#   respond_with(@user, status: :created)
#   display(@user, status: :ok)
#
# Results in:
#
#   render xml: @user, status: :created
#
def display(resource, given_options={})
  controller.render given_options.merge!(options).merge!(format => resource)
end
```

The navigational_behavior() implementation maps straight to the table in *Resource Status*, on page 108. For a GET request, it raises a missing-template error, because the only option for GET requests is to render a template, which we already tried and did not succeed with.

For other HTTP verbs, the navigational behavior checks whether the resource has errors. If so and a default action is given, it renders the default action specified by the DEFAULT_ACTIONS_FOR_VERBS hash. Finally, if the resource does not have errors, it redirects to the resource, which is what we expect in success cases.

The api_behavior() implementation goes through a different path. It uses the display() method, which merges the options given to respond_with() and adds a format before calling render. In other words, when we call respond_with() like this:

```
respond_with @user, status: :created
```

on GET requests for JSON format, the controller responds as follows:

```
render json: @user, status: :created
```

It's important to realize Rails responders do not call @user.to_json. They simply delegate this responsibility to the render() method and consequently to the :json renderer, as we saw in Section 1.2, *Writing the Renderer*, on page 5. This is important because people can add new renderers, and they work in responders without adding any other line of code.

Finally, the last customization available in responders can be done in our own controller. Imagine that we have a responder that works great in all cases, except for one specific action and format where we want it to behave differently. We can customize the responder for this scenario using the same block API as in respond_to():

```
def index
  @users = User.all
  respond_with(@users) do |format|
    format.json { render json: @users.to_json(some_specific_option: true) }
  end
end
```

And this all works because respond_with() forwards the block given to format.json to the responder when the request format is JSON. The default_render() seen in the previous responder snippets calls this block whenever the block is available.

The great advantage in using ActionController::Responder is that it centralizes how our application should behave per format. That said, if we want to change how all controllers behave at once, we just need to create our own responder and configure Rails to use it, as shown here:

```
ApplicationController.responder = MyAppResponder
```

Furthermore, we can set custom responders for specific controllers in our application:

```
class UsersController < ApplicationController
  self.responder = MyCustomUsersResponder
end
```

Let's create a responder with some extra behavior and configure Rails to use it.

6.3   The Flash Responder

The scaffolded controller uses flash messages in both create() and update() actions. These messages are quite similar across different controllers. Wouldn't it be nice if we could set these flash messages by default inside responders but still provide a nice API to change them?

Let's implement this feature using the internationalization framework (I18n) so we can easily look up flash messages from YAML files, configure default values, and make it possible to translate such messages in the future. Let's use rails plugin to create a new project called responders:

```
$ rails plugin new responders
```

Let's start by writing some tests that access create(), update(), and destroy() actions and ensure a flash message is being exhibited to the client:

responders/1_flash/test/responders/flash_test.rb
```
require "test_helper"
class FlashTest < ActionController::TestCase
  tests UsersController

  test "sets notice message on successful creation" do
    post :create, user: { name: "John Doe" }
    assert_equal "User was successfully created.", flash[:notice]
  end

  test "sets notice message on successful update" do
    user = User.create!(name: "John Doe")
    put :update, id: user.id, user: { name: "Another John Doe" }
    assert_equal "User was successfully updated.", flash[:notice]
  end

  test "sets notice message on successful destroy" do
    user = User.create!(name: "John Doe")
    delete :destroy, id: user.id
    assert_equal "User was successfully destroyed.", flash[:notice]
  end
end
```

The test relies on the existence of a UsersController, which we can define by invoking the scaffold generator inside the dummy application at test/dummy. When invoking the generator, let's skip the test files, guaranteeing they won't conflict with our plug-in tests:

```
$ rails g scaffold User name:string --no-test-framework
```

Next run migrations and set up our test database:

```
$ rake db:migrate db:test:clone
```

Notice, however, that the scaffold generator does not use the responder API. Let's change the generated controller to use respond_with() and then remove all flash messages, as our responders will set them automatically. This is our UsersController after these changes:

responders/1_flash/test/dummy/app/controllers/users_controller.rb
```ruby
class UsersController < ApplicationController
  respond_to :html, :json
  before_action :set_user, only: [:show, :edit, :update, :destroy]
  def index
    @users = User.all
    respond_with(@users)
  end
  def show
    respond_with(@user)
  end
  def new
    @user = User.new
    respond_with(@user)
  end
  def edit
  end

  def create
    @user = User.new(user_params)
    @user.save
    respond_with(@user)
  end

  def update
    @user.update(user_params)
    respond_with(@user)
  end

  def destroy
    @user.destroy
    respond_with(@user)
  end

  private
  # Use callbacks to share common setup or constraints between actions.
  def set_user
    @user = User.find(params[:id])
  end

  # Only allow a trusted parameter "white list" through.
  def user_params
    params.require(:user).permit(:name)
  end
end
```

All the actions in this controller should invoke respond_with(), with the exception of the edit() action. This is because the edit() action is used only by navigational requests, as its main responsibility is to show the form to edit the resource.

When we run the test suite, it fails with the following message:

```
1) Failure:
test_sets_notice_message_on_successful_creation(FlashTest):
Expected: "User was successfuly created."
  Actual: nil
```

The failure is expected because we haven't implemented our responders yet. Since we'll develop two responder extensions in this chapter, let's write each extension as a module, allowing developers to include such functionality wherever they desire. Our first module is called Responders::Flash, and it looks up flash messages via the I18n framework.

Imagine a request with valid parameters at the create() action in the UsersController. When respond_with() is called and no flash message is set, the responder should try to find an I18n message under the controller namespace and action, which in this case is "flash.users.create.notice". If an I18n message is found, the responder should set it in flash[:notice], and it will be properly exhibited in the next request.

Alternatively, if the request at UsersController#create does not have valid parameters (that is, the created user is invalid), the responder should search for a message at "flash.users.create.alert" and set flash[:alert] instead.

With these requirements in mind, let's write our Responders::Flash module:

```
responders/1_flash/lib/responders/flash.rb
module Responders
  module Flash
    def to_html
      set_flash_message! unless get?
      super
    end
    private
    def set_flash_message!
      status = has_errors? ? :alert : :notice
      return if controller.flash[status].present?

      message = i18n_lookup(status)
      controller.flash[status] = message if message.present?
    end

    def i18n_lookup(status)
      namespace = controller.controller_path.gsub("/", ".")
      action    = controller.action_name
```

```
        lookup  = [namespace, action, status].join(".").to_sym
        default = ["actions", action, status].join(".").to_sym
        I18n.t(lookup, scope: :flash, default: default,
               resource_name: resource.class.model_name.human)
      end
    end
end
```

Our module overwrites the to_html() behavior to set flash messages for non-GET requests and then calls super, allowing the responder behavior and other extensions to kick in.

Besides setting flash messages based in the controller namespace, our implementation gives an "actions" namespace as a :default option to I18n.t. This allows I18n to fall back to "flash.actions.create.notice" if a message cannot be found at "flash.users.create.notice".

This fallback mechanism lets us provide application-wide default messages so we don't need to repeat ourselves in each controller. Let's set the default scaffold messages inside our plug-in by simply creating a YAML file with the following:

responders/1_flash/lib/responders/locales/en.yml
```
en:
  flash:
    actions:
      create:
        notice: "%{resource_name} was successfully created."
        alert: ""
      update:
        notice: "%{resource_name} was successfully updated."
        alert: ""
      destroy:
        notice: "%{resource_name} was successfully destroyed."
        alert: "%{resource_name} could not be destroyed."
```

Now any controller will use the flash messages configured in this YAML file, unless we define a specific key for the controller to customize its message. To achieve this, we use I18n interpolation, which allows us to use %{resource_name} in our messages, and it will be replaced by the resource human name given to :resource_name when I18n.t is invoked.

To finally make our tests pass, we need to make our Responders::Flash available. Instead of monkey-patching the Rails default responder, let's inherit from it and add our own customizations. We'll set our new responders as the default ones and add our default YAML file with translations to I18n's load path:

responders/1_flash/lib/responders.rb
```
require "action_controller"
require "responders/flash"
module Responders
  class AppResponder < ActionController::Responder
    include Flash
  end
end

ActionController::Base.responder = Responders::AppResponder
require "active_support/i18n"
I18n.load_path << File.expand_path("../responders/locales/en.yml", __FILE__)
```

Run the test suite, and you'll see that our responder is properly triggered and is using the default flash messages in the YAML file! Since our tests only assert for "notice" messages, let's write one extra test asserting that "alert" messages will be shown in case of failures:

responders/1_flash/test/responders/flash_test.rb
```
test "sets alert messages from the controller scope" do
  begin
    I18n.backend.store_translations :en,
      flash: { users: { destroy: { alert: "Cannot destroy!" } } }

    user = User.create!(name: "Undestroyable")
    delete :destroy, id: user.id
    assert_equal "Cannot destroy!", flash[:alert]
  ensure
    I18n.reload!
  end
end
```

The test creates a resource and tries to destroy it, but fails, showing a message that the resource cannot be destroyed. As we did in *Aiming for an Active Model–Compliant API*, on page 21, we're using the I18n API to store translations on the fly for the failure scenario.

To make the test pass, let's add a before_destroy() callback that adds error messages to @user.errors and returns false if the username is "Undestroyable":

responders/1_flash/test/dummy/app/models/user.rb
```
class User < ActiveRecord::Base
  before_destroy do
    if name == "Undestroyable"
      errors.add(:base, "is undestroyable")
      false
    end
  end
end
```

We need to attach errors to the model to signal to the responder that something went wrong. With this final change, our tests pass again! There are other features we could add to our flash responder, but let's move on and make our responder a better HTTP citizen.

6.4 HTTP Cache Responder

Rails has embraced REST since version 1.2, and since then, developing APIs has become easier and easier. However, as your application grows, you may have to focus more on your API implementation and find ways to optimize the number of requests it can handle.

When you expose an API, it's common that a client requests a resource to the server several times, and the client always gets the same response back since the requested resource has not changed. In these cases, the server is wasting time rendering the same resource all over again, and the client is parsing the same response just to find out that nothing has changed.

Luckily, the HTTP 1.1 specification has a section dedicated to caching. The previous problem could be easily solved if the server appends a Last-Modified header to the response with a timestamp representing when the resource was last modified. For subsequent requests, the client should add an If-Modified-Since header with this timestamp, and if the resource has not changed, the server should return a 304 Not Modified status and does not need to render the resource again. Upon receiving a 304 status, the client knows that nothing has changed. Figure 13, *Client and server interaction with HTTP cache*, on page 120 illustrates this scenario.

As usual, let's start our implementation by writing tests. There are at least three scenarios to take into account:

- When If-Modified-Since is not provided, our controller responds normally but adds a Last-Modified header.

- When If-Modified-Since is provided and fresh, our controller responds with a status of 304 and a blank body.

- When If-Modified-Since is provided and not fresh, our controller responds normally but adds a new Last-Modified header.

To write these tests, we need to modify some request headers and verify that a few response headers are being properly set. Let's once again use the existing UsersController, available from the dummy app, to support our tests:

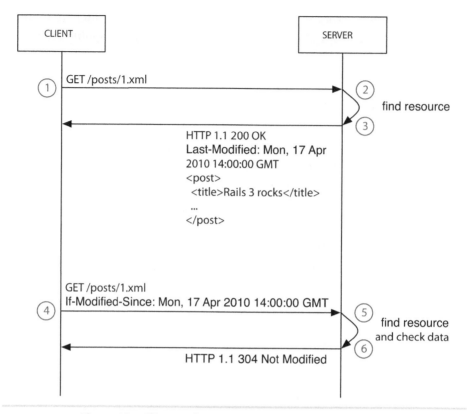

Figure 13—Client and server interaction with HTTP cache

responders/2_http_cache/test/responders/http_cache_test.rb
```ruby
require "test_helper"
class HttpCacheTest < ActionController::TestCase
  tests UsersController

  setup do
    @request.accept = "application/json"
    ActionController::Base.perform_caching = true

    User.create(name: "First", updated_at: Time.utc(2009))
    User.create(name: "Second", updated_at: Time.utc(2008))
  end

  test "responds with last modified using the latest timestamp" do
    get :index
    assert_equal Time.utc(2009).httpdate, @response.headers["Last-Modified"]
    assert_match '"name":"First"', @response.body
    assert_equal 200, @response.status
  end
```

```
  test "responds with not modified if request is still fresh" do
    @request.env["HTTP_IF_MODIFIED_SINCE"] = Time.utc(2009, 6).httpdate
    get :index
    assert_equal 304, @response.status
    assert @response.body.blank?
  end

  test "responds with last modified if request is not fresh" do
    @request.env["HTTP_IF_MODIFIED_SINCE"] = Time.utc(2008, 6).httpdate
    get :index
    assert_equal Time.utc(2009).httpdate, @response.headers["Last-Modified"]
    assert_match '"name":"First"', @response.body
    assert_equal 200, @response.status
  end
end
```

Rails provides several helpers on top of the HTTP cache specification, and we'll use them to create a new module called Responders::HttpCache that automatically adds HTTP cache functionality to all GET requests:

responders/2_http_cache/lib/responders/http_cache.rb
```
module Responders
  module HttpCache
    delegate :response, to: :controller
    def to_format
      return if do_http_cache? && do_http_cache!
      super
    end

    private

    def do_http_cache!
      response.last_modified ||= max_timestamp if max_timestamp
      head :not_modified if fresh = request.fresh?(response)
      fresh
    end

    # Iterate through all resources and find the last updated.
    def max_timestamp
      @max_timestamp ||= resources.flatten.map do |resource|
        resource.updated_at.try(:utc) if resource.respond_to?(:updated_at)
      end.compact.max
    end
    # Just trigger the cache if it's a GET request and
    # perform caching is enabled.
    def do_http_cache?
      get? && ActionController::Base.perform_caching
    end
  end
end
```

Our implementation mainly loops through all given resources and retrieves the timestamp of the last updated one. We then update the response object, and if the request is fresh (that is, if the resource was not modified in between requests), we return a 304 status to the client and don't render any resource, since to_format() returns before calling super.

Before running our new tests, let's require responders/http_cache and include Responders::HttpCache in our AppResponder, modifying the top of the lib/responders.rb file:

```
responders/2_http_cache/lib/responders.rb
require "responders/flash"
require "responders/http_cache"

module Responders
  class AppResponder < ActionController::Responder
    include Flash
    include HttpCache
  end
end
```

And that's it! Our test suite is green again! We extracted the flash and HTTP cache responsibility from our controllers, and now it's handled automatically by our responder!

6.5 More Ways to Customize Generators

Now that we understand how responders work and how to adapt them to our needs, we can feel confident about using them more and more in our controllers. The only issue is that the scaffold generator uses respond_to() by default, and not respond_with().

On the other hand, in *Generators' Hooks*, on page 74, we discussed how to customize generators, and there must be a hook to customize the controller generated in scaffold, right? Let's look at the scaffold's output:

```
invoke  active_record
create    db/migrate/20130415031520_create_users.rb
create    app/models/user.rb
invoke  resource_route
 route     resources :users
invoke  scaffold_controller
create    app/controllers/users_controller.rb
invoke    erb
create      app/views/users
create      app/views/users/index.html.erb
create      app/views/users/edit.html.erb
create      app/views/users/show.html.erb
```

```
create      app/views/users/new.html.erb
create      app/views/users/_form.html.erb
invoke   helper
create      app/helpers/users_helper.rb
invoke  assets
invoke   js
create      app/assets/javascripts/users.js
invoke   css
create      app/assets/stylesheets/users.css
invoke  css
create    app/assets/stylesheets/scaffold.css
```

Each invoke in the output is a hook that we can overwrite. This means we can indeed replace the scaffold_controller generator with another one that fits our needs.

However, this is not how we'll solve this problem. Instead, let's use another Rails-generator feature to customize templates without a need to use generator hooks.

Generators' Source Path

Consider the following line in a Rails generator:

```
copy_file "controller.rb", "app/controller/#{file_name}_controller.rb"
```

It simply copies the controller.rb file from the generators' source to the given destination, which for a UsersController would be app/controllers/users_controller.rb.

However, a generator can have more than one source! Before copying a file to a given location, the generator searches for this source file in several locations, called *source paths*. The source_root() class method we specified in *Creating Our First Generator*, on page 77, is actually the last place a generator searches for a template.

This behavior is built into Thor,[1] but Rails wraps the behavior nicely by automatically adding the lib/templates directory inside your application to all generators' source paths. This means the Rails::Generators::ScaffoldControllerGenerator used in the scaffold will always try to find a template at lib/templates/rails/scaffold_controller before using the one Rails provides.

When we look at the implementation of Rails::Generators::ScaffoldControllerGenerator in the Rails source code, we can easily see the logic that copies the controller template:

---

1. https://github.com/wycats/thor

rails/railties/lib/rails/generators/rails/scaffold_controller/scaffold_controller_generator.rb
```ruby
module Rails
  module Generators
    class ScaffoldControllerGenerator < NamedBase
      def create_controller_files
        template "controller.rb", File.join("app/controllers", class_path,
          "#{controller_file_name}_controller.rb")
      end
    end
  end
end
```

It uses a template named controller.rb, which is available at railties/lib/rails/genera-tors/rails/scaffold_controller/templates/controller.rb. According to the source paths, if we place a file at lib/templates/rails/scaffold_controller/controller.rb inside our application, Rails will use this application file instead of the one that ships with Rails!

You can easily try this by creating a new Rails application, placing an empty file in lib/templates/rails/scaffold_controller/controller.rb inside your application, and running the scaffold command. When you check the controller the scaffold creates, it's empty!

Let's use this awesome feature to customize the scaffold to use respond_with() by default.

Using respond_with by Default

To use respond_with() by default in the scaffold, let's place a template in our application's lib/templates. However, to avoid doing this in each new application, we'll create a generator that copies a file to the proper location.

Let's call this generator Responders::Generators::InstallGenerator and implement it as follows:

responders/3_final/lib/generators/responders/install/install_generator.rb
```ruby
module Responders
  module Generators
    class InstallGenerator < Rails::Generators::Base
      source_root File.expand_path("../templates", __FILE__)
      def copy_template_file
        copy_file "controller.rb",
          "lib/templates/rails/scaffold_controller/controller.rb"
      end
    end
  end
end
```

Here is the template our generator uses:

responders/3_final/lib/generators/responders/install/templates/controller.rb

```ruby
<% module_namespacing do -%>

class <%= controller_class_name %>Controller < ApplicationController
  before_action :set_<%= singular_table_name %>,
    only: [:show, :edit, :update, :destroy]

  # GET <%= route_url %>
  def index
    @<%= plural_table_name %> = <%= orm_class.all(class_name) %>
    respond_with(@<%= plural_table_name %>)
  end

  # GET <%= route_url %>/1
  def show
    respond_with(@<%= singular_table_name %>)
  end

  # GET <%= route_url %>/new
  def new
    @<%= singular_table_name %> = <%= orm_class.build(class_name) %>
    respond_with(@<%= singular_table_name %>)
  end

  # GET <%= route_url %>/1/edit
  def edit
  end

  # POST <%= route_url %>
  def create
    @<%= singular_table_name %> = <%= orm_class.build(class_name,
                                      "#{singular_table_name}_params") %>
    @<%= orm_instance.save %>
    respond_with(@<%= singular_table_name %>)
  end

  # PATCH/PUT <%= route_url %>/1
  def update
    @<%= orm_instance.update("#{singular_table_name}_params") %>
    respond_with(@<%= singular_table_name %>)
  end

  # DELETE <%= route_url %>/1
  def destroy
    @<%= orm_instance.destroy %>
    respond_with(@<%= singular_table_name %>)
  end

  private
```

```
# Use callbacks to share common setup or constraints between actions.
def set_<%= singular_table_name %>
  @<%= singular_table_name %> = <%= orm_class.find(class_name, "params[:id]") %>
end

# Only allow a trusted parameter "white list" through.
def <%= "#{singular_table_name}_params" %>
  <%- if attributes_names.empty? -%>
  params[<%= ":#{singular_table_name}" %>]
  <%- else -%>
  params.require(<%= ":#{singular_table_name}" %>).
    permit(<%= attributes_names.map { |name| ":#{name}" }.join(', ') %>)
  <%- end -%>
  end
end
<% end -%>
```

The previous template is based on the one that ships with Rails, but it replaces all respond_to() calls with respond_with(). It also uses several methods we've already discussed, except orm_class() and orm_instance(), which we'll cover soon.

To try the new generator, simply move to the dummy application and invoke it:

```
$ rails g responders:install
```

Now when you scaffold any new resource, it will use the template we just installed! This means the Rails scaffold is flexible not only for Rails extensions like Haml or RSpec, but also for application developers, because they can customize the scaffold to fit their workflow, application structure, and markup.

Generators and ORM Agnosticism

We already discussed Active Model and its role in ORM agnosticism. We also talked about generator hooks, which provide a way for other ORMs to hook into model and scaffold generators. Whenever we use the scaffold generator, those two roles intersect and Rails provides a custom API to allow ORMs to customize the generated code.

Rails controllers are responsible for interacting with the model and passing the desired objects to the view. In other words, controllers should interact with the current ORM and retrieve the required information from it. The controller generated by scaffolding should change depending on the ORM used. Rails solves this problem by creating an object responsible for telling the scaffold generator how the interaction with the ORM happens. The basic implementation for this object is available in the Rails source code, and it looks like this:

```
rails/railties/lib/rails/generators/active_model.rb
module Rails
  module Generators
    class ActiveModel
      attr_reader :name
      def initialize(name)
        @name = name
      end
      # GET index
      def self.all(klass)
        "#{klass}.all"
      end

      # GET show
      # GET edit
      # PATCH/PUT update
      # DELETE destroy
      def self.find(klass, params=nil)
        "#{klass}.find(#{params})"
      end
      # GET new
      # POST create
      def self.build(klass, params=nil)
        if params
          "#{klass}.new(#{params})"
        else
          "#{klass}.new"
        end
      end

      # POST create
      def save
        "#{name}.save"
      end
      # PATCH/PUT update
      def update(params=nil)
        "#{name}.update(#{params})"
      end
      # POST create
      # PATCH/PUT update
      def errors
        "#{name}.errors"
      end
      # DELETE destroy
      def destroy
        "#{name}.destroy"
      end
    end
  end
end
```

The orm_class() points to Rails::Generators::ActiveModel, and orm_instance() points to an instance of this same class. So, whenever we invoke orm_class.all("User") in the template, it invokes Rails::Generators::ActiveModel.all("User") and returns User.all, which is the normal Active Record behavior.

The orm_instance() behaves similarly, except we don't need to pass the resource name as an argument, since we already did that in initialization. For this reason, orm_instance.save successfully returns user.save for Active Record.

All interaction between the controller and the ORM is specified in Rails::Generators::ActiveModel. The agnosticism comes from the fact that any ORM can provide its own implementation of this class. We only need to define an Active Model class inside the ORM's generator namespace.

For example, DataMapper has different syntax for finding and updating records. So, it needs to inherit from Rails::Generators::ActiveModel and implement the new API:

```
module DataMapper
  module Generators
    class ActiveModel < ::Rails::Generators::ActiveModel
      def self.find(klass, params=nil)
        "#{klass}.get(#{params})"
      end
    end
  end
end
```

The structure generators provide, along with the Active Model API, make agnosticism possible in Rails, allowing developers to choose the tools that best fit their workflow.

6.6 Wrapping Up

In this chapter, we looked into responders to understand how they work and how to customize them. As a proof of concept, we developed two extensions for responders, one to handle flash messages and another to handle HTTP caching.

There is much more we could delegate to responders. In the HTTP layer, we could use the If-Unmodified-Since request-header to provide conditional PUT requests, wherein the resource is updated only if it's not modified after the given date; otherwise, we return a 409 Conflict status. Figure 14, *Client and server interaction with HTTP conditional requests*, on page 129 shows this scenario.

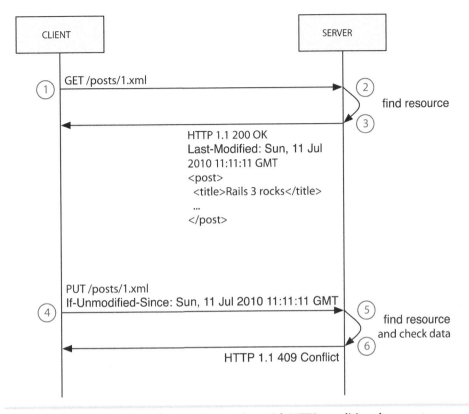

CLIENT

SERVER

① GET /posts/1.xml

② find resource

③

HTTP 1.1 200 OK
Last-Modified: Sun, 11 Jul
2010 11:11:11 GMT
<post>
 <title>Rails 3 rocks</title>
 ...
</post>

④ PUT /posts/1.xml
If-Unmodified-Since: Sun, 11 Jul 2010 11:11:11 GMT

⑤ find resource
and check data

⑥

HTTP 1.1 409 Conflict

Figure 14—Client and server interaction with HTTP conditional requests

We also took another look at Rails generators and learned more about ORM agnosticism.

If you want to bring responders and respond_with() to your workflow, you may want to try the Responders gem by Plataformatec,[2] which implements both extensions developed in this chapter and contributes some extra features, such as the ability to change responders to redirect to the index() action instead of the show() action when a user is created or updated.

Next let's hook into Rails's Notifications API to store all queries Rails sends to the database, and use a Rails mountable engine to expose those queries through a web interface isolated from our application!

---

2.   https://github.com/plataformatec/responders

In this chapter, we'll see
- ActiveSupport::Notifications API
- Rails mountable and isolated engines
- Rack, middleware stacks, and custom middleware

## CHAPTER 7

Managing Application Events with Mountable Engines

Since Ruby on Rails's early days, people have wondered what happens inside of their applications. How many queries were performed in this request? How long did this request take?

To address this common concern, a few open source projects (such as Footnotes and Bullet[1,2]) and services (such as Scout and New Relic's RPM[3,4]) were built. Since all those different tools needed to extract this information from Rails, Rails evolved to provide a centralized way to publish and subscribe to events happening inside an application with the ActiveSupport::Notifications application programming interface (API).

In this chapter, we'll use this API to subscribe to all actions processed by our application and store them in a MongoDB database. Then we'll use a Rails engine to create a set of routes, controllers, and views to navigate through the stored data. This engine can then be shared between Rails applications and mounted at specific endpoints.

7.1 Mountable and Isolated Engines

In Chapter 5, *Streaming Server Events to Clients Asynchronously*, on page 83, we created a Rails engine that streams data to our application. In addition to providing a controller, the engine added new routes to our application, and helper methods like live_assets. In a way, that engine was directly extending

---

1. https://github.com/josevalim/rails-footnotes
2. https://github.com/flyerhzm/bullet
3. http://scoutapp.com/
4. http://www.newrelic.com/features.html

our Rails application with its own components. However, this behavior is not always desirable.

Take for instance the plug-in we'll build in this chapter. It's going to provide its own models, controllers, and views. As the plug-in grows, the number of routes will start to multiply, as will the number of helper methods. If our plug-in implements a show_paginated_results() helper and a Rails application uses our plugin, we don't want our helper to be available inside the Rails application, since the helper is internal to our plugin. Even worse, if the application has its own show_paginated_results() helper, it would override the helper defined in our plugin, which can lead to failures!

Rails solves those issues by providing mountable and isolated engines. A mountable engine uses its own router instead of adding routes directly to the application router. An isolated engine is built inside its own namespace, with its own models, controllers, views, assets, and helpers. Let's generate our first mountable engine with the rails plugin command, passing --mountable as an option:

```
$ rails plugin new mongo_metrics --mountable
```

The --mountable option generates a mountable and isolated engine. We can observe this by checking a couple of different files. First, let's open up the plug-in's config/routes.rb:

mongo_metrics/1_engine/config/routes.rb
```
MongoMetrics::Engine.routes.draw do
end
```

Notice how the routes are drawn through the engine. Compare them to the config/routes.rb generated in rake Section 5.1, *Extending Rails with Engines*, on page 84, which are drawn directly on the application:

live_assets/1_live/config/routes.rb
```
Rails.application.routes.draw do
  get "/live_assets/:action", to: "live_assets"
end
```

Since the routes are no longer added to the application, the engine needs to be explicitly mounted in the application router, which is done automatically by the rails plugin command in the test/dummy application:

mongo_metrics/1_engine/test/dummy/config/routes.rb
```
Rails.application.routes.draw do
  mount MongoMetrics::Engine => "/mongo_metrics"
end
```

That's all it takes to make our engine mountable. To have an isolated engine, we need to explicitly declare it as isolated and choose a namespace. The --mountable option automatically generates an engine definition with MongoMetrics as the isolated namespace:

```
mongo_metrics/1_engine/lib/mongo_metrics/engine.rb
module MongoMetrics
  class Engine < ::Rails::Engine
    isolate_namespace MongoMetrics
  end
end
```

Because we're declaring an isolated namespace, all of our controllers, models, and helpers should be defined *inside* this namespace, guaranteeing they will be isolated from the rest of the application. Now helper files defined in the engine won't be automatically included by the application and vice versa. It also sets up many conveniences—for example, if we were using Active Record, it would prefix all model table names with mongo_metrics_ and ensure Rails generates namespaced models, controllers, and helpers.

Besides those changes, the rails plugin command with the --mountable option generates a couple of extra files, like assets manifests and a MongoMetrics::ApplicationController at app/controllers/mongo_metrics/application_controller.rb, making our engine closer to how a brand-new Rails application would look.

With our plug-in setup ready, it's time to explore Rails's ActiveSupport::Notifications API and start storing those notifications in the database.

7.2 Storing Notifications in the Database

Before we implement the logic to store notifications in the database, let's look at the Notifications API.

The Notifications API

The Notifications API consists of just two methods: instrument() and subscribe(). The former is called when we want to instrument and publish an event, and for Action Controller processing, it looks like this:

```
ActiveSupport::Notifications.instrument("process_action.action_controller",
    format: :html, path: "/", action: "index") do
  process_action("index")
end
```

The first argument is the name of the event published, which in this case is process_action.action_controller, and the second is a hash with information about the event, called payload. To subscribe to those notifications, we just need to pass the event name and a block to subscribe(), as follows:

```
event = "process_action.action_controller"
ActiveSupport::Notifications.subscribe(event) do |*args|
  # do something
end
```

where args is an array with five items:

- name: A String with the name of the event

- started_at: A Time object representing when the event started

- ended_at: A Time object representing when the event ended

- instrumenter_id: A String containing the unique ID of the object instrumenting the event

- payload: A Hash with the information given as payload to the instrument() method

And that's all we need to know. Next let's take a look at the database where we'll store the notifications.

Using MongoDB

MongoDB is a fast and document-oriented database perfectly suited to storing notifications since it's high-volume, low-value data. You can read more about MongoDB at its website,[5] which also includes installation instructions for different operating systems.

Currently, there are several object-relational mappers to interact with MongoDB, and we'll use Mongoid for this project.[6] We won't cover installation instructions, so if you don't have MongoDB installed, please do it now! After MongoDB is installed and running, let's add Mongoid as a dependency to our plugin:

mongo_metrics/1_engine/mongo_metrics.gemspec
```
s.add_dependency "mongoid", "~> 4.0.0"
```

Let's also generate the Mongoid configuration inside our test/dummy application:

```
$ rails g mongoid:config
```

and require mongoid as soon as we load up our metrics plug-in:

---

5.   http://www.mongodb.org/

6.   http://mongoid.org/

```
mongo_metrics/1_engine/lib/mongo_metrics.rb
require "mongoid"
require "mongo_metrics/engine"

module MongoMetrics
end
```

With Mongoid configured, let's create our first model, properly namespaced at app/models/mongo_metrics/metric.rb:

```
mongo_metrics/1_engine/app/models/mongo_metrics/metric.rb
module MongoMetrics
  class Metric
    include Mongoid::Document
  end
end
```

Before writing any logic that stores documents in MongoDB, let's write a test in test/mongo_metrics_test.rb. The test instruments an event with the name process_action.action_controller and asserts a metric was stored in MongoDB with all relevant fields:

```
mongo_metrics/1_engine/test/mongo_metrics_test.rb
require "test_helper"

class MongoMetricsTest < ActiveSupport::TestCase
  setup { MongoMetrics::Metric.delete_all }

  test "process_action notification is saved in the mongo database" do
    event   = "process_action.action_controller"
    payload = { "path" => "/" }

    ActiveSupport::Notifications.instrument event, payload do
      sleep(0.001) # simulate work
    end

    metric = MongoMetrics::Metric.first
    assert_equal 1, MongoMetrics::Metric.count
    assert_equal event, metric.name
    assert_equal "/", metric.payload["path"]

    assert metric.duration
    assert metric.instrumenter_id
    assert metric.started_at
    assert metric.created_at
  end
end
```

When we run the test, it fails since we are not storing anything yet:

```
1) Failure:
test_process_action_notification_is_saved_in_the_mongo_database(MongoMetricsTest)
Expected: 1
  Actual: 0
```

To make the test pass, let's first subscribe to ActiveSupport::Notifications at the end of lib/mongo_metrics.rb:

```ruby
require "active_support/notifications"

module MongoMetrics
  EVENT = "process_action.action_controller"
  ActiveSupport::Notifications.subscribe EVENT do |*args|
    MongoMetrics::Metric.store!(args)
  end
end
```

Our notification hook is simply calling the store!() method in our MongoMetrics::Metric, which will be responsible for parsing the arguments and creating a record in the database, as follows:

```ruby
module MongoMetrics
  class Metric
    include Mongoid::Document

    field :name, type: String
    field :duration, type: Integer
    field :instrumenter_id, type: String
    field :payload, type: Hash
    field :started_at, type: DateTime
    field :created_at, type: DateTime

    def self.store!(args)
      metric = new
      metric.parse(args)
      metric.save!
    end

    def parse(args)
      self.name            = args[0]
      self.started_at      = args[1]
      self.duration        = (args[2] - args[1]) * 1000000
      self.instrumenter_id = args[3]
      self.payload         = args[4]
      self.created_at      = Time.now.utc
    end
  end
end
```

After this change, our test suite is green! To look at how our plug-in works outside the test environment, let's create a controller HomeController with three actions inside test/dummy and then boot the dummy application:

```
$ rails g controller Home foo bar baz
$ rails s
```

Now make a few requests over /home/foo, /home/bar, and /home/baz to generate some data. When you're done, start a new console session with rails console and see all notifications created by these requests by typing MongoMetrics::Metric.all.to_a in the command line.

Although our subscriber works as expected, wouldn't it be nice if we had a page where we could see these notifications instead of using the Rails console? Let's harness the power provided by Rails engines once again!

The Notifications Page

To create our notifications page, let's create a controller, a view, and routes inside our engine. We'll start with the controller:

mongo_metrics/2_metrics/app/controllers/mongo_metrics/metrics_controller.rb

```
module MongoMetrics
  class MetricsController < ApplicationController
    respond_to :html, :json

    def index
      @metrics = Metric.all
      respond_with(@metrics)
    end

    def destroy
      @metric = Metric.find(params[:id])
      @metric.destroy
      respond_with(@metric)
    end
  end
end
```

Our controller has two actions: index() and destroy(). For the first one, we need to create a view:

mongo_metrics/2_metrics/app/views/mongo_metrics/metrics/index.html.erb

```
<h1>Listing Metrics</h1>

<table>
  <tr>
    <th>Name</th>
    <th>Duration</th>
    <th>Started at</th>
```

```
      <th>Payload</th>
      <th></th>
  </tr>
  <%= content_tag_for :tr, @metrics do |metric| %>
    <td><%= metric.name %></td>
    <td><%= metric.duration / 1000 %>ms</td>
    <td><%= time_ago_in_words metric.started_at %> ago</td>
    <td>
      <ul>
      <% metric.payload.each do |k, v| %>
        <li><%= k.humanize %>: <%= v %></li>
      <% end %>
      </ul>
    </td>
    <td><%= link_to 'Destroy', metric_path(metric),
        method: :delete, data: { confirm: 'Are you sure?' } %></td>
  <% end %>
</table>
```

For the Destroy links in our view to work in the browser, we need to add the jquery-rails gem as a dependency:

mongo_metrics/2_metrics/mongo_metrics.gemspec
```
s.add_dependency "jquery-rails", "~> 3.0.1"
```

then require the dependency at the top of lib/mongo_metrics.rb, as we did for mongoid:

mongo_metrics/2_metrics/lib/mongo_metrics.rb
```
require "jquery-rails"
```

then require both jquery and jquery_ujs in the javascript manifest file:

mongo_metrics/2_metrics/app/assets/javascripts/mongo_metrics/application.js
```
//= require jquery
//= require jquery_ujs
//= require_tree .
```

Finally, let's add some routes at config/routes.rb:

mongo_metrics/2_metrics/config/routes.rb
```
MongoMetrics::Engine.routes.draw do
  root to: "metrics#index"
  resources :metrics, only: [:index, :destroy]
end
```

Notice how we declared the routes without worrying about namespaces. Since our engine is mountable and isolated, Rails saves us the trouble of specifying the namespace on every route. Furthermore, in our view, we simply called metric_path() and Rails automatically looked up this route in the engine router and not in the application router. Even if the application had a metric_path() named route, the routes wouldn't conflict!

However, this raises a question: what if we want to access an application route from the engine, or an engine route from the application?

To illustrate the issue, we'll write integration tests. Our tests need to access a couple of pages in the dummy application and then go over our plug-in pages to guarantee the notifications are being exhibited properly:

```
mongo_metrics/2_metrics/test/integration/navigation_test.rb
require "test_helper"
class NavigationTest < ActionDispatch::IntegrationTest
  setup { MongoMetrics::Metric.delete_all }

  test "can visualize notifications" do
    get main_app.home_foo_path
    get main_app.home_bar_path
    get main_app.home_baz_path

    get mongo_metrics.root_path
    assert_match "Path: /home/foo", response.body
    assert_match "Path: /home/bar", response.body
    assert_match "Path: /home/baz", response.body
  end

  test "can destroy notifications" do
    get main_app.home_foo_path
    metric = MongoMetrics::Metric.first
    delete mongo_metrics.metric_path(metric)
    assert_empty MongoMetrics::Metric.where(id: metric.id)
  end
end
```

Our new tests should pass right off the bat. Notice that every time we want to access an application page, we use the main_app() proxy and the mongo_metrics() proxy for the mountable engine pages. The Rails application will always be accessible through main_app(); the name of the engine proxy can be found by running rake routes in the dummy application:

```
      Prefix Verb URI Pattern            Controller#Action
    home_foo GET /home/foo(.:format) home#foo
    home_bar GET /home/bar(.:format) home#bar
    home_baz GET /home/baz(.:format) home#baz
mongo_metrics     /mongo_metrics       MongoMetrics::Engine

Routes for MongoMetrics::Engine:
   root GET    /                       mongo_metrics/metrics#index
metrics GET    /metrics(.:format)      mongo_metrics/metrics#index
 metric DELETE /metrics/:id(.:format) mongo_metrics/metrics#destroy
```

The name of the proxy is under the Prefix column. Notice rake routes conveniently shows the routes of the mounted engine, as well! If desired, you can also boot up the dummy app and access the notifications page in your browser.

Now that we're properly storing and exhibiting information from MongoDB, we can see that every time we access our engine pages, it also stores data in MongoDB. It would be impractical if we turned off the metrics storage every time we accessed the plug-in itself. To solve this problem, let's provide a mechanism to mute notifications in some selected places. To do that, we need to understand how Rails integrates with Rack.

7.3 Rails and Rack

Quoting the Rack documentation:[7]

> Rack provides a minimal, modular, and adaptable interface for developing web applications in Ruby. By wrapping HTTP requests and responses in the simplest way possible, it unifies and distills the API for web servers, web frameworks, and software in between (the so-called middleware) into a single method call.

Rails applications need a web server in order to interact through the HTTP protocol. And since the early days, the Rails community has seen a huge range of web servers available to deploy applications.

Early on, Rails was responsible for providing an adapter to each web server it supported: one for Mongrel, another for WEBrick, another for Thin, and so on. Similarly, other frameworks had to provide different adapters for the same web servers since they had a different API than Rails.

This quickly proved to be a duplication of efforts, and at the beginning of 2007, Rack was released with the goal of unifying the APIs used by web servers and web frameworks. By following the Rack API, a web framework could use Rack web-server adapters instead of providing its own, removing the duplication of effort that exists in the Ruby community.

Although Rails 2.2 already provided a simple Rack interface, Rails more closely embraced Rack and its API in version 2.3. However, the Rack revolution really happened in Rails 3, where several parts of Rails became Rack endpoints, and you could easily mount different Rack applications in the same process. For example, we can easily mount a Sinatra application inside the Rails router, similar to how we mounted an engine inside the dummy application in this chapter.

---

7.   http://rack.rubyforge.org/doc/

Hello, Rack!

The Rack specification clearly outlines the API that Rack applications use to communicate with a web server and between themselves:[8]

> A Rack application is any Ruby object that responds to call. It takes exactly one argument, the environment, and returns an array of exactly three values: the status, the headers, and the body.

Rack's minimal API allows us to write a simple web application in just a few lines of code:

```
require 'rack'
class HelloRack
  def call(env)
    [200, { 'Content-Type' => 'text/html' }, ['Hello Rack!']]
  end
end
run HelloRack.new
```

By creating the previous config.ru file in a directory and invoking the rackup command inside this same directory, Rack starts a web server and invokes our HelloRack application in each request. When you fire up a browser and type in *http://localhost:9292/*, you can see "Hello Rack!" returned as the response body.

All Rails applications ship with a config.ru file, as we can see in the dummy application inside test/dummy, with the following contents:

```
# This file is used by Rack-based servers to start the application.
require ::File.expand_path('../config/environment', __FILE__)
run Rails.application
```

Every Rails application is also a Rack application: it implements the call() method, which receives the environment and returns an array with three elements. By default, its implementation sends the request to the application router (the one defined in config/routes.rb), which dispatches the request to another Rack application if any route matches. Let's explore further.

Understanding the Rails Router

The Rails router can dispatch to any Rack application:

```
Rails.application.routes.draw do
  match "/hello", to:
    lambda { |env| [200, { "Content-Type" => "text/plain" }, ["World"]] }
end
```

---

8. http://rack.rubyforge.org/doc/SPEC.html

When we add this route to any Rails application and type /hello in the browser, we get "World" as the response from the server. In fact, when we have a route like this:

```
Rails.application.routes.draw do
  match "/hello", to: "posts#index"
end
```

Rails, before a request, automatically converts controller#action to a Rack application. You can retrieve any action from a controller as a Rack application by simply doing this:

```
PostsController.action(:index)
PostsController.action(:index).responds_to?(:call) # => true
```

Whenever you call get(), post(), put(), delete(), resources(), or resource() in the router domain-specific language, those methods invoke to the match() method. The only method that has different semantics is mount(), used in the dummy application to mount our engine.

The match() method works by matching the full route. If we think in terms of regular expressions, when we say match "/mongo_metrics", it only matches paths as %r"\A/mongo_metrics\z" (the query string is not considered in matches). However, when mounting an engine or any other Rack application, we don't match requests to only /mongo_metrics, but also to /mongo_metrics/metrics, /mongo_metrics/other, and so on. The equivalent regular expression would be %r"\A/mongo_metrics", without the \z anchor.

You may have noticed there is something more going on. To access the mounted engine, we issue requests to /mongo_metrics/metrics, but the engine router matches only on /metrics, ignoring the /mongo_metrics prefix. Why?

Whenever a request hits a Rack server, the server gets the request path, stores it in the environment hash as env["PATH_INFO"], and passes it down to the underlying Rack application. Mounting works because, when dispatching to a mounted engine, Rails removes /mongo_metrics from env["PATH_INFO"], so the engine sees only /metrics (as if a browser were accessing /metrics straight in the engine).

This mechanism works not only with engines, but with any Rack application, since this is outlined in the Rack specification itself. The specification also dictates that Rails should set env["SCRIPT_NAME"] = "/mongo_metrics" before calling the mounted engine. This tells the engine it is mounted at a specific point, allowing the engine to still generate full URLs.

To sum it up, we have a Rails application, which is a Rack application, that invokes our router, which is another Rack application, that finally dispatches to another Rack application—a controller and action, an engine, or even a Sinatra application. It's Rack applications all the way! And to make things even more interesting, Rack provides the concept of middleware, which allows us to add custom code between those Rack applications, giving us even more flexibility. We'll explore that next.

7.4 Middleware Stacks

Although web-server adapters and the Rack application API revolutionized the way Ruby web frameworks are developed, you're probably more familiar with another term related to Rack: *middleware*.

A middleware wraps around a Rack application. It lets us manipulate both the request sent down to the application and the response the application returns. By piling up many middleware before an application, we create a *middleware stack*. Any request to an action in a Rails controller passes through three middleware stacks, as the following figure shows.

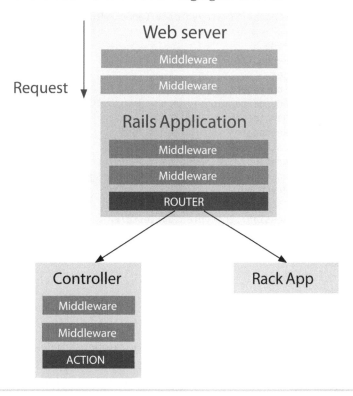

Figure 15—The middleware stacks involved in a request to an action in a Rails controller

Rails hides the first of these three middleware stacks. It sits between the web server and the Rails::Application object and contains only two middleware components:

- Rails::Rack::LogTailer: Parses the log file and prints it on the console
- Rails::Rack::Debugger: Requires and enables debugger

After passing through this middleware stack, the request hits a Rails::Application (for example, our Dummy::Application inside test/dummy), which is nothing more than another middleware stack with the router sitting at the end.

The stack that the Rails::Application contains is the most known middleware stack in Rails. You can add or remove middleware from this stack through config.middlewares, available inside config/application.rb. To see all available middleware in the stack, we need to invoke rake middleware from the command line at the application root.

For our dummy application inside test/dummy, rake middleware returns the following:

```
use ActionDispatch::Static
use Rack::Lock
use #<ActiveSupport::Cache::Strategy::LocalCache::Middleware:0x007fed3d5eddf0>
use Rack::Runtime
use Rack::MethodOverride
use ActionDispatch::RequestId
use Rails::Rack::Logger
use ActionDispatch::ShowExceptions
use ActionDispatch::DebugExceptions
use ActionDispatch::RemoteIp
use ActionDispatch::Reloader
use ActionDispatch::Callbacks
use ActiveRecord::Migration::CheckPending
use ActiveRecord::ConnectionAdapters::ConnectionManagement
use ActiveRecord::QueryCache
use ActionDispatch::Cookies
use ActionDispatch::Session::EncryptedCookieStore
use ActionDispatch::Flash
use ActionDispatch::ParamsParser
use Rack::Head
use Rack::ConditionalGet
use Rack::ETag
use Rack::Mongoid::Middleware::IdentityMap
run Dummy::Application.routes
```

The middleware stack will change based on your dependencies and your Rails environment. For example, Rack::Mongoid::Middleware::IdentityMap is a Mongoid dependency, whereas ActionDispatch::Reloader is usually available only in development. Let's run down the list of middleware:

- ActionDispatch::Static: Serves public assets in development.

- Rack::Lock: Wraps a Mutex around the application so just one thread can access it at a given time. When we set config.allow_concurrency to true in Section 5.3, *Filesystem Notifications with Threads*, on page 92, we instructed Rails to remove this middleware.

- ActiveSupport::Cache::Strategy::LocalCache: Uses an in-memory cache store to provide a local cache during requests.

- Rack::Runtime: Measures the request time and returns it as an X-Runtime header.

- Rack::MethodOverride: Checks POST requests and converts them to PUT or DELETE if _method is present in parameters.

- ActionDispatch::RequestId: Sets the request ID information, which is shown in logs.

- Rails::Rack::Logger: Logs each request

- ActionDispatch::DebugExceptions and ActionDispatch::ShowExceptions: Is responsible for showing helpful error pages in development and rendering status pages in production from the public directory.

- ActionDispatch::RemoteIp: Handles IP spoof–checking.

- ActionDispatch::Callbacks and ActionDispatch::Reloader: Run the to_prepare callbacks—once on application boot in production, and before each request in development (such as I18n and route reloading).

The next three middleware are all related to Active Record, followed by middleware responsible for managing cookies, session, and flash messages. The last few middleware are as follows:

- ActionDispatch::ParamsParser: Parses the parameters given in the request, both from a query string or in the POST body

- Rack::Head: Converts HEAD requests to GET requests

- Rack::ConditionalGet: Returns a 304 status code in case the appropriate HTTP cache headers match

- Rack::ETag: Calculates the digest of the response body using the MD5 algorithm and sets it as the HTTP response ETag header

The last stop in the stack is the application router, which is yet another Rack application. If the router dispatches the request to a specific action in a controller, it'll also pass through another middleware stack since each controller has its own middleware stack. We can add a middleware to a controller as follows:

```
class UsersController < ApplicationController
  use MyMiddleware
  use AnotherMiddleware
end
```

The controller middleware stack is invoked before any filters and before the action is processed. As Rails provides many options to hook up a middleware, a middleware seems to be a good choice to implement the mechanism that turns off our metrics store, so let's write our first middleware!

Building the **MuteMiddleware**

Before writing our middleware, we need to ensure MongoMetrics provides a method to mute notifications for a specific block of code. Let's call this method mute!() and provide a mute?() that returns true whenever notifications are muted. Let's write a test:

mongo_metrics/3_final/test/mongo_metrics_test.rb
```
test 'can ignore notifications when specified' do
  MongoMetrics.mute! do
    assert MongoMetrics.mute?
    event = "process_action.action_controller"
    ActiveSupport::Notifications.instrument event do
      sleep(0.001) # simulate work
    end
  end
  assert !MongoMetrics.mute?
  assert_equal 0, MongoMetrics::Metric.count
end
```

To make our test pass, let's implement these two methods and change the block passed to subscribe to respect the mute condition:

mongo_metrics/3_final/lib/mongo_metrics.rb
```
require "mongoid"
require "jquery-rails"
require "mongo_metrics/engine"
require "active_support/notifications"
module MongoMetrics
  EVENT = "process_action.action_controller"
  ActiveSupport::Notifications.subscribe EVENT do |*args|
    MongoMetrics::Metric.store!(args) unless mute?
  end

  def self.mute!
    Thread.current["sql_metrics.mute"] = true
    yield
  ensure
    Thread.current["sql_metrics.mute"] = false
  end
```

```ruby
  def self.mute?
    Thread.current["sql_metrics.mute"] || false
  end
end
```

Notice we used thread variables to ensure that muting a request in a thread won't affect other threads in a threaded environment. Also, we need to wrap the yield() call in an ensure block, allowing the mute status to be reverted even if an exception happens while executing the block. Let's write a test for it, too:

mongo_metrics/3_final/test/mongo_metrics_test.rb
```ruby
test 'does not leak mute state on failures' do
  MongoMetrics.mute! do
    assert MongoMetrics.mute?
    raise "oops"
  end rescue nil

  assert !MongoMetrics.mute?
end
```

With our mute!() implementation ready, we can write the MuteMiddleware. To guarantee our middleware works as expected, let's write an integration test that asserts that accessing our metrics controller doesn't generate any event:

mongo_metrics/3_final/test/integration/navigation_test.rb
```ruby
test "does not log engine actions" do
  get mongo_metrics.root_path
  assert 0, MongoMetrics::Metric.count
end
```

Any Rack middleware is initialized with the application or the middleware it should call next in the stack. Whenever our MuteMiddleware middleware is invoked, it only has to invoke the underlying application inside a mute!() block, effectively muting everything happening downstream. Let's implement it:

mongo_metrics/3_final/lib/mongo_metrics/mute_middleware.rb
```ruby
module MongoMetrics
  class MuteMiddleware
    def initialize(app)
      @app = app
    end

    def call(env)
      MongoMetrics.mute! { @app.call(env) }
    end
  end
end
```

Since a usual Rails request goes through three different middleware stacks, we need to evaluate the best place to use our middleware:

- A stack between the web server and the Rails application is inaccessible, so it is out of the question.

- A stack inside the application that finishes with the router isn't appropriate since adding our middleware to this stack would mute *all* requests.

- A stack inside each controller is our best option since we can add it directly to MongoMetrics::ApplicationController.

However, when a request goes to an engine, there is another middleware stack sitting between the application router and the engine router; it's the engine's own middleware stack, as the following figure shows.

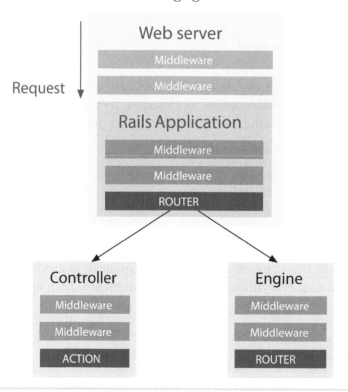

Figure 16—All the middleware stacks involved in a request that includes a Rails engine

This middleware stack is similar to a Rails application stack, but empty by default. If we add our middleware to the engine stack, any request that goes to our metrics plug-in, regardless of the controller, will be automatically muted. That seems handy; let's add our middleware to this stack:

```
mongo_metrics/3_final/lib/mongo_metrics/engine.rb
require "mongo_metrics/mute_middleware"

module MongoMetrics
  class Engine < ::Rails::Engine
    isolate_namespace MongoMetrics
    config.middleware.use MuteMiddleware
  end
end
```

We can configure the engine middleware stack via config.middleware. If we were inside a Rails application, we would have used config.middleware too. config.middleware always points to the current engine's or application's middleware stack. If we wanted to modify the application middleware stack from the engine, we could access it via config.app_middleware.

After those changes, our tests will be green once again. By using middleware, we can easily disable metrics storage for specific sections of our plug-ins and applications. If we want to disable it for a specific controller in an application, or even for specific actions, we can do so:

```
class AdminController < ApplicationController
  # You could also use :only and :except options.
  # use MuteControllerMiddleware, only: :index
  use MuteControllerMiddleware
end
```

Every time a Rack application is involved, it is trivial to add a middleware stack around it, and Rails does it often to provide different points for us to extend our applications.

Trimming Down the Middleware Stack

When we executed rake middleware in the dummy application, it contained a bunch of middleware related to Active Record. In fact, our plug-in has a dependency on the rails gem, which depends on Active Record and other gems, like Action Mailer, that we're not using. Let's break our rails dependency in the gemspec into two smaller ones:

```
mongo_metrics/3_final/mongo_metrics.gemspec
s.add_dependency "railties", "~> 4.0.0"
s.add_dependency "sprockets-rails", "~> 2.0.0"
```

The rails gem is a "meta gem." It doesn't ship with any code; instead, it simply contains Rails's default stack as a dependency. That's why it depends on Active Record, Action Mailer, Sprockets, and more. In our case, we've replaced the rails gem with the railties gem, which is Rails's backbone containing the booting processes, railties, engine and application definitions, as well as the sprockets-rails, which allows us to serve our assets. The railties gem already depends on actionpack (for routes, controllers, and views) and on activesupport (Ruby extensions), so we don't need to add them explicitly.

After making those changes, our application will no longer boot since our application configuration files were generated expecting some of the removed dependencies to be present. That said, be sure to remove any config.active_record and config.action_mailer from the environment files at test/dummy/config/environments. Also, check your test files to ensure you don't have any calls related to fixtures, like fixtures :all, in the test/integration/navigation_test.rb.

If you run rake middleware once again, Active Record middleware will no longer be in our stack. The process we've just completed is similar to how we would have trimmed down dependencies in a Rails application. The main step is to replace the rails gem in the Gemfile by direct dependencies and then clean up the application configuration files. We can even remove some components, such as Sprockets and Active Record, when generating the application or the plug-in; we simply pass --skip-sprockets or --skip-active-record when invoking rails new or rails plugin new.

7.5 Streaming with Rack

Although we could improve our metrics application to show beautiful graphics and reports, we will instead provide a way to export the data stored in the database so it can be rendered in a third-party service or tool.

The default approach to send data from the server to the client in Rails is to use the send_data() method. However, this approach requires us to generate upfront the whole string we want to send, which may take time and require a lot of memory as we store more metrics in our database. To solve this problem, we'll stream data, allowing us to send data to the client in chunks without allocating a huge blob of memory.

In Chapter 5, *Streaming Server Events to Clients Asynchronously*, on page 83, we used Rails's live-streaming facilities to stream data from the server. Now we'll rely solely on the Rack specification's flexibility to implement this feature. Our streaming format of choice is CSV because a client can consume the data row by row and Ruby has built-in tools to convert data to CSV.

Streaming Redux

The Rack specification outlines that a valid response body is any Ruby object that responds to the method each(). That's why we commonly use arrays in Rack applications to hold the response body:

```
class HelloRack
  def call(env)
    [200, { 'Content-Type' => 'text/html' }, ['Hello Rack!']]
  end
end
```

The Rack web server will loop over the response body, using the each() method, and output the data yielded. Since the array responds to each(), it yields once with value "Hello Rack!"

This API contract means we can implement streaming in Rack by simply having a custom response body that implements a custom iteration mechanism via each(). Here's how we could implement streaming using only Rack:

```
require 'rack'

class StreamingRack
  def call(env)
    [200, { 'Content-Type' => 'text/html' }, self]
  end
  def each
    while true
      yield 'Hello Rack!\n'
    end
  end
end
run StreamingRack.new
```

Write the previous code to a config.ru file and then run rackup -s puma to boot the Rack application. Let's once again use cURL through the command line and see data streaming through:[9]

```
$ curl -v localhost:9292/
```

And that's it! Streaming data with Rack is quite accessible. Press CTRL+C to shut down the Rack application and the cURL process.

CSV Streamer

Let's start our CSV-streamer implementation by writing a test that accesses the metrics path with .csv, and get the CSV document back from the server:

mongo_metrics/3_final/test/integration/navigation_test.rb
```
test "exports data to csv" do
  get main_app.home_foo_path
  get mongo_metrics.metrics_path(format: :csv)
  assert_match "process_action.action_controller,", response.body
end
```

---

9.   http://curl.haxx.se/

Because the route that handles the CSV request is already defined, we just need to change the MongoMetrics::MetricsController controller to respond to CSV requests on the index action. Our index() already uses respond_with(), so the following should be enough to get a CSV response back:

```
mongo_metrics/3_final/app/controllers/mongo_metrics/metrics_controller.rb
module MongoMetrics
  class MetricsController < ApplicationController
    respond_to :html, :json
    respond_to :csv, only: :index
```

However, recall the discussion from Section 6.2, *Exploring ActionController::Responder*, on page 109; Rails will first try to render a template, which does not exist, and then fall back to calling render csv: @metrics. The issue here is that Rails does not implement a CSV renderer, so we need to write it ourselves. Luckily, we discussed how to write renderers in Chapter 1, *Creating Our Own Renderer*, on page 1.

We want our CSV renderer to send a file back to the user, streaming each chunk little by little. The renderer should also set the response body to be a custom object, which we'll call CSVStreamer. Let's implement it:

```
mongo_metrics/3_final/lib/mongo_metrics/csv_streamer.rb
module MongoMetrics
  ActionController::Renderers.add :csv do |model, options|
    headers = self.response.headers
    headers["Content-Disposition"] =
      %(attachment; filename="#{controller_name}.csv")
    headers["Cache-Control"] = "no-cache"
    headers.delete "Content-Length"
    self.content_type ||= Mime::CSV
    self.response_body  = CSVStreamer.new(model)
  end
  class CSVStreamer
    def initialize(scope)
      @scope = scope
    end
    def each
      @scope.each do |record|
        yield record.to_csv
      end
    end
  end
end
```

First we set the Content-Disposition header to tell the browser we're sending an attachment. Second, we turn off the cache and remove the Content-Length, notifying the underlying Rack server that we want to stream the data. Finally, we assign the proper content type and set the response body to our custom CSVStreamer object.

Notice our streamer object calls to_csv() on each metrics record, so we need to implement to_csv(), too. Since Ruby provides a library named csv to generate and consume CSV in its standard library, let's require it and use it to convert an array with metrics information to CSV:

```
mongo_metrics/3_final/app/models/mongo_metrics/metric.rb
require "csv"
def to_csv
  [name, started_at, duration, instrumenter_id, created_at].to_csv
end
```

The last step to make our test pass is to require mongo_metrics/csv_streamer, the file where we defined our custom CSV renderer, making it available to our controllers:

```
mongo_metrics/3_final/lib/mongo_metrics.rb
require "mongo_metrics/csv_streamer"
```

Our new test now passes! Although the implementation of CSV streaming with Rack is a bit different from how we would implement it using ActionController::Live, it suffers from the same limitations and requires the same care when deployed. We were able to test our endpoint because we weren't streaming infinitely, unlike with our project in Chapter 5, *Streaming Server Events to Clients Asynchronously*, on page 83.

So, which option should we choose to implement streaming: ActionController::Live or Rack streaming? In general, live streaming is preferable. Because Rack streaming relies on Rack's basic API, a web server doesn't know up front which kind of response it will send back—long (streaming) or short (regular)—making it hard for web servers to optimize such scenarios. Live streaming, on the other hand, is a Rails abstraction that can evolve transparently from the developer code as Rack improves the underlying streaming functionality. In any case, streaming with Rack may be convenient for small Rack applications that do not have access to all the conveniences Rails provides.

This particular feature could even be implemented without streaming, simply by using one of the many background processing tools available to Rails, such as Delayed Job and Resque, to generate the CSV file in the background and send an email once it is done.[10,11]

---

10. https://github.com/collectiveidea/delayed_job
11. https://github.com/resque/resque

7.6 Wrapping Up

In this chapter, we developed a Rails engine that listens to all actions an application processes, and stores them in MongoDB. We can see these notifications by accessing /mongo_metrics in the browser.

Our implementation was built atop a mountable and isolated engine, which allows us to build our features isolated from a Rails application, guaranteeing we won't have conflicts in the most likely places, such as routes and helpers. We also explored Rack by creating middleware that allows us to mute the metrics storage on particular areas of our plug-in and by using a custom Rack body to stream data.

There's still a lot to be done in our plug-in when it comes to the visualization part. We could, for instance, allow the developer to sort metrics by duration and provide charts. Even more interestingly, we could use the streaming techniques we've covered so far to stream events to the visualization page as they happen.

Next let's create a Rails application that allows us to translate I18n messages through a Sinatra app authenticated with Devise, a popular authentication library.

In this chapter, we'll see
 • The I18n framework
 • The Sinatra web framework
 • The Rails router
 • Devise (for authentication) and Capybara (for integration
   testing) gems

CHAPTER 8

Translating Applications
Using Key-Value Back Ends

The internationalization framework (I18n) added in Rails 2.2 played a key role in increasing Rails adoption around the world. Although we can easily make an application available in different languages, the biggest issue is maintaining this translation data. Some companies have a team of translators available, while others choose a collaborative approach and allow their own users to translate the web app. In both cases, it is common to develop a web interface to aid with the translation process.

By default I18n stores translation data in YAML files, which can be difficult to manipulate through the web interface. In fact, using YAML would require a mechanism to tell all servers to sync and reload the YAML files once they're updated. As you can imagine, such a solution could grow in complexity quickly.

Luckily, the I18n framework comes with different back ends that allow us to store translations in places other than YAML files. This makes it much easier to manipulate the translations table through a web interface and update the site translations on demand. There is no need to synchronize YAML files between web servers. On the downside, retrieving translations from the database instead of an in-memory hash has a huge impact on performance.

A key-value store is a solution that can comply with both the simplicity and performance requirements. In this chapter, we'll store translations in a Redis store and use a key-value back end to retrieve them. Additionally, we'll build a simple Sinatra application to expose a web interface to read, create, and update these translations on the fly.[1]

Unlike in previous chapters, we'll develop all this functionality as a Rails application instead of a plug-in. After studying and analyzing railties and engines, we can now build Rails applications with a different perspective.

8.1 Revisiting Rails::Application

In previous chapters, we discussed Rails::Engine and how it exhibits several behaviors similar to a Rails application. When we look at the Rails source code, we find the following:

```
module Rails
  class Application < Engine
    # ...
  end
end
```

The Rails::Application class inherits from Rails::Engine! This means an application can do everything an engine does, plus has some specific behavior:

- An application is responsible for all bootstrapping (for example, loading Active Support, setting up load paths, and configuring the logger).

- An application has its own router and middleware stack (as we discussed in Section 7.4, *Middleware Stacks*, on page 143).

- An application should load and initialize all plug-ins.

- An application is responsible for reloading code and routes between requests if they changed.

- An application is responsible for loading tasks and generators when appropriate.

To take a closer look at these responsibilities, let's start developing our Translator app:

```
$ rails new translator
```

When we studied the dummy application in Chapter 1, *Creating Our Own Renderer*, on page 1, we discussed the responsibilities of the config/boot.rb, config/application.rb, and config/environment.tb files. In particular, the boot file is responsible for setting our load paths, the application file defines our Rails application, and the environment file finally initializes the app by calling the initialize!() method:

1.　http://www.sinatrarb.com/

translator/1_app/config/environment.rb
```
# Load the rails application.
require File.expand_path('../application', __FILE__)

# Initialize the rails application.
Translator::Application.initialize!
```

In *Initializers*, on page 86, we showed how engines provide a set of initializers that drive how the engine boots. It's no surprise that a Rails application provides such initializers too:

```
module Translator
  class Application < Rails::Application
    initializer "translator.say_hello" do
      puts "hello on initialization"
    end
  end
end
```

To see all initializers available in a Rails application, open a Rails console on our newly generated app and type the following:

```
Rails.application.initializers.map(&:name)
```

The difference here is that the application contains not only its own initializers, but also the initializers defined on all railties and engines. Initializing a Rails application is just a matter of executing those initializers one by one.

Everything else in a Rails application is built around the boot, application, and environment files. If we open the Rakefile, we'll see the following:

translator/1_app/Rakefile
```
require File.expand_path('../config/application', __FILE__)
Translator::Application.load_tasks
```

First, the application file is required, defining the Rails application. Next, load_tasks() is invoked, loading all Rake tasks provided by the application, plug-ins, and Rails itself. Note that we don't require the environment file at any point. This allows basic rake commands to run fast since they don't initialize the application; they just define it.

However, many tasks need the application to be initialized. For example, rake db:migrate works only if the database is configured. That's why Rails provides a Rake task called :environment; this task merely requires config/environment.rb to initialize our application. Whenever you need to access the database or any of your application classes in a Rake task, you need to depend on the :environment task.

Finally, let's look at config.ru in the root of our application. It requires the environment file, effectively initializing the application, and runs the current Rails application as a Rack application:

translator/1_app/config.ru
```
# This file is used by Rack-based servers to start the application.

require ::File.expand_path('../config/environment', __FILE__)
run Rails.application
```

The application initialization process is broken into many files, but only because we need to hook into different points. The config.ru file needs the whole environment up front, whereas Rakefile loads it in steps. However, nothing is stopping us from merging all these files into a single-file Rails application!

The Single-File Rails Application

Bundling a Rails application into a single file helps us understand how to set up and initialize Rails. Let's look at a sample single-file Rails application and discuss it next. Create an empty directory and add a config.ru file with the following contents:

translator/config.ru
```
# We will simply use rubygems to set our load paths
require "rubygems"
# Require our dependencies
require "rails"
require "active_support/railtie"
require "action_dispatch/railtie"
require "action_controller/railtie"

class SingleFile < Rails::Application
  # Set up production configuration
  config.eager_load = true
  config.cache_classes = true

  # A key base is required for our app to boot
  config.secret_key_base = "pa34u13hsleuowilaisejkez12u39201pluaep2ejlkwhkj"

  # Define a basic route
  routes.append do
    root to: lambda { |env|
      [200, { "Content-Type" => "text/plain" }, ["Hello world"]]
    }
  end
end

SingleFile.initialize!
run Rails.application
```

We can initialize this application by running rackup in the same directory as the config.ru. Open your browser at *localhost:9292*, and you should get "Hello world" back!

A single-file Rails application is not much different from a regular Rails application. It sets up the load path, in this case by simply using RubyGems instead of Bundler. Then it loads all dependencies one by one instead of using require "rails/all", usually found at the top of config/application.rb. Finally, it defines, initializes, and runs the application.

Note that Rails requires us to define some configuration options, such as the confsig.secret_key_base. All this is already familiar to us; the only new method used in this file is routes.append.

In general, the only method Rails developers access on the router is draw(), as found in a config/routes.rb file:

```
Translator::Application.routes.draw do
  # ...
end
```

The draw() method is meant to work with code reloading. Every time a route file changes, all previously drawn routes are cleared and they are redrawn from scratch by reloading all config/routes.rb entries in the application and plug-ins. However, in some cases, some routes may be defined during initialization or inside a file that is never reloaded. For such scenarios, Rails provides both routes.prepend and routes.append to define sticky routes.

For example, if you use routes.draw to define routes inside config/application.rb, which is not reloaded in development, as soon as your routes are reloaded because you changed something in config/routes.rb, the routes defined in the application will effectively be lost.

A request to this single-file Rails application works as in any other Rails application. The web server invokes the SingleFile#call() method, passing through a middleware stack that ends with the router. In our case, the router simply matches on the root action to a custom Rack application.

Since we now understand the application responsibilities and how it's built on top of railties and engines, it's time to move back to the Translator app and create our translation back end using the I18n API.

8.2 I18n Back Ends and Extensions

Whenever we invoke I18n.translate() (also aliased as I18n.t()) or I18n.localize() (also aliased as I18n.l()) in our application, it is delegating these methods to the I18n back end stored in I18n.backend(). By replacing this back end, you can completely modify how the I18n library works. The I18n framework ships with three different back ends:

- I18n::Backend::Simple: Keeps translations in an in-memory hash populated from YAML files; this is the default back end.

- I18n::Backend::KeyValue: Uses any key-value store as a back end, as long it complies with a minimum API.

- I18n::Backend::Chain: Allows you to chain several back ends; in other words, if a translation cannot be found in one back end, it searches for it in the next back end in the chain.

Rails relies on many features I18n provides. For example, in our translator app, we can see the following line in config/environments/production.rb:

```
config.i18n.fallbacks = true
```

Whenever this configuration option is set to true, Rails configures the I18n framework to *include* the fallbacks functionality in the current back end, allowing any lookup to fall back to the default locale if a translation cannot be found in the current locale. If you're using I18n outside of a Rails application, you can also use the fallbacks behavior with one line of code:

```
I18n.backend.class.send(:include, I18n::Backend::Fallbacks)
```

Another I18n feature Rails uses is transliteration support. The transliteration that ships with Rails allows you to replace accented Latin characters with their correspondent unaccented ones, as shown here:

```
I18n.transliterate("dziękuję") # => "dziekuje"
```

If you need to transliterate Hebraic, Cyrillic, Chinese, or other characters, you can add new transliteration rules on demand. Keep in mind that fallbacks and transliterations are not a back end, but rather one of the several extensions listed here, provided by the I18n library:

- I18n::Backend::Cache: Uses a cache store in front of I18n.t to store translation results; that is, the string after lookup, interpolation, and pluralization took place.

- I18n::Backend::Cascade: Cascades lookups by removing nested scopes from the lookup key; in other words, if :"foo.bar.baz" cannot be found, it automatically searches for :"foo.bar".

- I18n::Backend::Fallbacks: Provides locale fallbacks, falling back to the default locale if a translation cannot be found in the current one.

- I18n::Backend::Gettext: Provides support to gettext and .po files.

- I18n::Backend::InterpolationCompiler: Compiles interpolation keys (like %{model}) into translation data to speed up performance.

- I18n::Backend::Memoize: Memoizes lookup results; in contrast to I18n::Backend::Cache, it uses an in-memory hash and is useful if you are using the key-value back end.

- I18n::Backend::Metadata: Adds metadata (such as pluralization count and interpolation values) to translation results.

- I18n::Backend::Pluralization: Adds support to pluralization rules under :"i18n.plural.rule".

- I18n::Backend::Transliterator: Adds support to transliteration rules (as discussed earlier) under :"i18n.transliterate.rule".

The I18n library provides several back ends and extensions for different areas, such as improving performance or adding more flexibility for languages with specific needs, such as custom pluralization. In this chapter, we'll use just two of them: I18n::Backend::KeyValue and I18n::Backend::Memoize.

The key-value back end for I18n can accept any object as a store, as long as it complies with the following API:

- @store[]: A method to read a value given a key
- @store[]=: A method to set a value given a key
- @store.keys: A method to retrieve all stored keys

Since providing a compliant API is trivial, almost all key-value stores can be used with this back end. In this chapter, let's use Redis since it is generally available and is used widely in production.[2]

After Redis is installed and running, let's integrate it with our Rails application by adding the redis gem,[3] a pure-Ruby client library for Redis, to our Gemfile:

translator/1_app/Gemfile
```
gem 'redis', '~> 3.0.3'
```

And then install the added gem:

```
bundle install
```

Now let's fire up a Rails console with rails console and check that Redis conforms with the API that I18n expects:

---

2. http://redis.io
3. https://github.com/redis/redis-rb

```
db = Redis.new
db["foo"] = "bar"
db["foo"] # => bar
db.keys   # => ["foo"]
```

Going back to our I18n setup, let's create a file called lib/translator.rb, which will be responsible for setting up a Redis instance pointing to the appropriate database (the database is referenced as an integer in Redis). Let's also create a customized key-value back end that includes the I18n::Backend::Memoize module to cache lookups and uses the Redis store on initialization:

translator/1_app/lib/translator.rb
```ruby
module Translator
  DATABASES = {
    "development" => 0,
    "test" => 1,
    "production" => 2
  }

  def self.store
    @store ||= Redis.new(db: DATABASES[Rails.env.to_s])
  end

  class Backend < I18n::Backend::KeyValue
    include I18n::Backend::Memoize

    def initialize
      super(Translator.store)
    end
  end
end
```

Next, let's configure the I18n framework to use our new back end at Translator::Application:

translator/1_app/config/application.rb
```ruby
module Translator
  class Application < Rails::Application
    # Set translator backend for I18n
    require "translator"
    config.i18n.backend = Translator::Backend.new
```

In contrast to the default I18n back end, the key-value back end does not load translations from YAML files before each request, but rather on demand (since it would be slow). That said, to store all default translations in our Redis store, we just need to execute the following command in a terminal:

```
$ rails runner "I18n.backend.load_translations"
```

When we start the Rails console again, we can access all new translations stored in our Redis store:

```
db = Translator.store
db.keys
db["en.errors.messages.blank"] # => "can't be blank"
db["en.number.precision"] # => "{\"format\":{\"delimiter\":\"\"}}"
```

Notice that the key-value store automatically encodes the values to JavaScript Object Notation (JSON).

8.3 Rails and Sinatra

With translations properly stored, we can now write our Translator app using Sinatra. Sinatra is a domain-specific language (DSL) for quickly creating web applications in Ruby with minimal effort. The "Hello world" is just a few lines of code:

```
# myapp.rb
require 'sinatra'
get '/' do
  'Hello world!'
end
```

We won't access the Sinatra application directly, but we'll integrate it with our Rails app. This allows us to reuse all the structure we already have in the Rails ecosystem, such as tests, sessions, authentication, and so on. Before we develop our Sinatra application, let's write an integration test once again using Capybara to make our tests more robust and readable. First, let's define ActiveSupport::IntegrationCase inside our test/test_helper.rb, which includes Capybara's DSL:

translator/1_app/test/test_helper.rb
```
require "capybara"
require "capybara/rails"
# Define a bare test case to use with Capybara
class ActiveSupport::IntegrationCase < ActiveSupport::TestCase
  include Capybara::DSL
  include Rails.application.routes.url_helpers
end
```

Our test-case definition is exactly the same as the one we used back in Section 2.2, *Integration Tests with Capybara*, on page 28. Now add Capybara to the Gemfile:

translator/1_app/Gemfile
```
group :test do
  gem 'capybara', '~> 2.0.0'
end
```

Our test attempts to localize a date using the Polish locale, but will fail because we don't have any translation data for this locale. Next, we should visit the translation URL /translator/en/pl, meaning we want to translate messages from English to Polish, then fill in the appropriate translation field and store this new translation. After that, we can assert that our translation was success-fully stored because we're able to localize a date. The implementation goes like this:

translator/1_app/test/integration/translator_app_test.rb
```ruby
require "test_helper"

class TranslatorAppTest < ActiveSupport::IntegrationCase
  # Set up store and load default translations
  setup { Translator.reload! }

  test "can translate messages from a given locale to another" do
    assert_raise I18n::MissingTranslationData do
      I18n.l(Date.new(2010, 4, 17), locale: :pl)
    end

    visit "/translator/en/pl"
    fill_in "date.formats.default", with: %{"%d-%m-%Y"}
    click_button "Store translations"

    assert_match "Translations stored with success!", page.body
    assert_equal "17-04-2010", I18n.l(Date.new(2010, 4, 17), locale: :pl)
  end
end
```

Our test setup invokes a method called Translator.reload!(). This method will be responsible for removing all keys from the database and reloading the trans-lation data. Let's implement it next:

translator/1_app/lib/translator.rb
```ruby
def self.reload!
  store.flushdb
  I18n.backend.load_translations
end
```

Our tests are ready to run with rake test, but they fail because our Sinatra application is not built yet. So, let's add both Sinatra and Haml to our project Gemfile (and install these new dependencies with bundle install):

translator/1_app/Gemfile
```ruby
gem 'sinatra', '~> 1.4.2', require: 'sinatra/base'
gem 'haml', '~> 4.0.2'
```

Our Sinatra application should define a route as /:from/:to, which, when accessed, renders a view with all translation data available in the :from locale, ready to be translated to the :to locale. Our first code iteration for our Sinatra application is shown here:

```
translator/1_app/lib/translator/app.rb
module Translator
  class App < Sinatra::Base
    set :environment, Rails.env
    enable :inline_templates

    get "/:from/:to" do |from, to|
      exhibit_translations(from, to)
    end

    protected

    # Store from and to locales in variables and retrieve
    # all keys available for translation.
    def exhibit_translations(from, to)
      @from, @to, @keys = from, to, available_keys(from)
      haml :index
    end

    # Get all keys for a locale. Remove the locale from the key and sort them.
    # If a key is named "en.foo.bar", this method will return it as "foo.bar".
    def available_keys(locale)
      keys  = Translator.store.keys("#{locale}.*")
      range = Range.new(locale.size + 1, -1)
      keys.map { |k| k.slice(range) }.sort!
    end

    # Get the value in the translator store for a given locale. This method
    # decodes values and checks if they are a hash, as we don't want subtrees
    # available for translation since they are managed automatically by I18n.
    def locale_value(locale, key)
      value = Translator.store["#{locale}.#{key}"]
      value if value && !ActiveSupport::JSON.decode(value).is_a?(Hash)
    end
  end
end
__END__

@@ index
!!!
%html
  %head
    %title
      Translator::App
  %body
    %h2= "From #{@from} to #{@to}"
```

```
%p(style="color:green")= @message

- if @keys.empty?
  No translations available for #{@from}
- else
  %form(method="post" action="")
    - @keys.each do |key|
      - from_value = locale_value(@from, key)
      - next unless from_value
      - to_value = locale_value(@to, key) || from_value
      %p
        %label(for=key)
          %small= key
          = from_value
        %br
        %input(id=key name=key type="text" value=to_value size="120")
    %p
      %input(type="submit" value="Store translations")
```

There are a few things to discuss in this implementation. First, notice we explicitly forward the Rails environment to the Sinatra application environment. Next, we define the /:from/:to route available through the request method GET. If a route matches, Sinatra will yield both parameters to the block, which will be executed. The block simply invokes exhibit_translations(), which assigns these parameters to instance variables, gets all locale keys available for translation, and renders the index template.

In this case, we chose to use Haml as template markup for the index page.[4] The template is just a few lines of code and was defined in the same file as the application via Sinatra's inline templates feature, which we enabled at the top of the application. However, it's important to notice that templates are evaluated in the same context as the application. This means any method defined in our Sinatra application is also available in the template, as are the application's instance variables. This approach is different from that in Rails, because Rails templates are not evaluated in the same context as controllers, but rather in a specific view context, so Rails needs to copy all instance variables from controllers to views behind the scenes, as we saw in Section 1.3, *Understanding the Rails Rendering Stack*, on page 9, and controller methods should be called explicitly as controller.method().

Finally, notice our template calls the locale_value() method. This method receives a locale and a key and returns the value stored in Redis. This method should

---

4. Haml stands for HTML Abstraction Markup Language, and you can find some examples at http://haml-lang.com/.

also handle hashes, which are created and stored by default by the I18n framework, to allow you to retrieve subtrees from back ends.

In I18n, whenever you store a translation { "foo.bar" => "baz" }, it decomposes the "foo.bar" key and stores { "foo" => { "bar" => "baz"} } as the translation. This allows you to retrieve either the specific translation with I18n.t("foo.bar") #=> "bar" or a subtree hash with I18n.t("foo") #=> { "bar" => "baz" }. That said, if we show hashes in our Sinatra interface, several translations would be duplicated because they would appear either in the subtree hash in the foo key, or in the full key foo.bar.

Before we try our Sinatra application, let's autoload it from lib/translator.rb, as shown here:

translator/1_app/lib/translator.rb
```
autoload :App, "translator/app"
```

And finally, let's mount it in the router at "translator":

translator/1_app/config/routes.rb
```
Translator::Application.routes.draw do
  mount Translator::App, at: "/translator"
end
```

Let's verify this now works by starting the server using rails server as usual and accessing /translator/en/pl in the browser. We get a translation page similar to the one in the following figure.

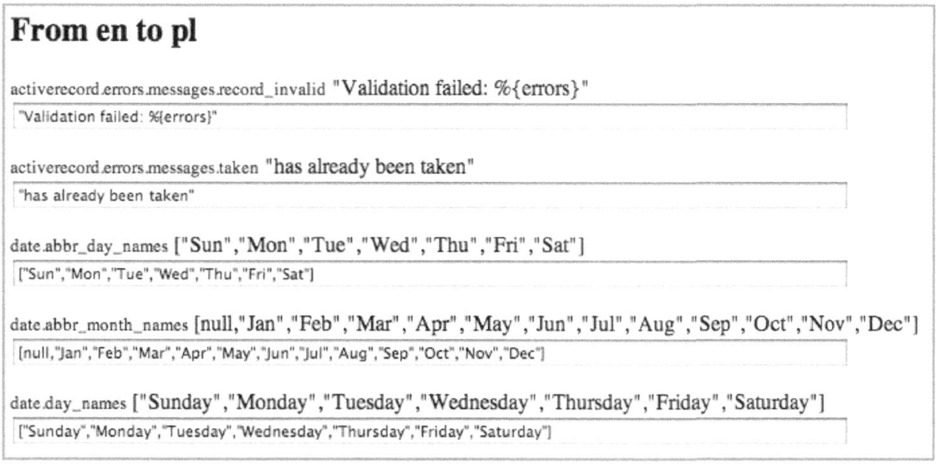

From en to pl

activerecord.errors.messages.record_invalid "Validation failed: %{errors}"

"Validation failed: %{errors}"

activerecord.errors.messages.taken "has already been taken"

"has already been taken"

date.abbr_day_names ["Sun","Mon","Tue","Wed","Thu","Fri","Sat"]

["Sun","Mon","Tue","Wed","Thu","Fri","Sat"]

date.abbr_month_names [null,"Jan","Feb","Mar","Apr","May","Jun","Jul","Aug","Sep","Oct","Nov","Dec"]

[null,"Jan","Feb","Mar","Apr","May","Jun","Jul","Aug","Sep","Oct","Nov","Dec"]

date.day_names ["Sunday","Monday","Tuesday","Wednesday","Thursday","Friday","Saturday"]

["Sunday","Monday","Tuesday","Wednesday","Thursday","Friday","Saturday"]

Figure 17—Translator app

This page automatically sets up a page to translate a message from English to Polish, but don't click the Submit button yet; we still haven't implemented the POST behavior. In fact, when we run the tests again, they fail for this reason. Clicking the button in integration tests returns a "No route matches" error:

```
1) Error:
test_can_translate_messages_from_a_given_locale_to_another(TranslatorAppTest)
  ActionController::RoutingError: No route matches [POST] "/translator/en/pl"
```

To make the test pass, let's add a new route to Sinatra for POST requests. This new route should store the translation in the I18n back end, passing the destination locale and the translations decoded from JSON to Ruby; call save() in the Redis store, forcing it to be dumped to the filesystem; and exhibit the translation page once again:

`translator/2_final/lib/translator/app.rb`
```ruby
post "/:from/:to" do |from, to|
  I18n.backend.store_translations to, decoded_translations, escape: false
  Translator.store.save
  @message = "Translations stored with success!"
  exhibit_translations(from, to)
end
protected
# Get all translations sent through the form and decode
# their JSON values to check validity.
def decoded_translations
  translations = params.except("from", "to")
  translations.each do |key, value|
    translations[key] = ActiveSupport::JSON.decode(value) rescue nil
  end
end
```

Notice we set :escape to false when storing translations so I18n can properly generate subtrees. By default, if you give a translation as { "foo.bar" => "baz" }, I18n will treat it as a single key, escaped as { "foo\000.bar" => "baz" }. When it's stored this way, we cannot retrieve its subtree as I18n.t("foo"). However, if we turn escaping to false, I18n will break the key apart, converting it to { "foo" => { "bar" => "baz" } } and allowing us to retrieve it as I18n.t("foo") or I18n.t("foo.bar").

Feel free to restart the server and translate all data from any locale to another! Notice I chose to represent the data as JSON in the interface, because we can easily represent arrays, strings, numbers, or Booleans.

At this point, all our tests are green! Our translator application is almost ready; now it's time to add authentication with Devise and improve the robustness of our tests with Capybara!

8.4 Taking It to the Next Level with Devise and Capybara

If any of our applications are going to provide an interface for translations, we should make sure this interface is password-protected and that we can properly test its functionality. In this section, let's look at Devise,[5] a full-stack authentication solution based on Rack, and take a deeper look at how we can use Capybara to test Rack applications.[6]

Adding Cross-Application Authentication

Devise is an interesting solution for authentication because it provides, in very few lines of code, a whole authentication stack, with sign-in, sign-up, password recovery, and more. It uses Warden to move the authentication handling to the middleware stack,[7] allowing any application, whether it's Sinatra or a Rails controller, to use the same authentication rules.

To add Devise to our Translator app, we first need to add it to our Gemfile and run bundle install to install it:

translator/2_final/Gemfile
```
gem 'devise', '~> 3.0.0'
```

With the gem installed in our machine, we need to invoke the devise:install generator:

```
$ rails g devise:install
```

The generator copies to our application a locale file and an initializer with several configuration options. At the end, it also prints some steps we need to do manually.

The first step is to configure Action Mailer for development:

translator/2_final/config/environments/development.rb
```
config.action_mailer.default_url_options = { host: 'localhost:3000' }
```

Then we add flash messages to our layout:

translator/2_final/app/views/layouts/application.html.erb
```
<p class="notice"><%= notice %></p>
<p class="alert"><%= alert %></p>
```

And finally we add a root route:

translator/2_final/config/routes.rb
```
root to: "home#index"
```

---

5. http://devise.plataformatec.com.br/
6. https://github.com/jnicklas/capybara
7. https://github.com/hassox/warden

Since our root route points to a HomeController, let's implement that controller. For now, the index action just renders a link to the mounted Sinatra application:

```
translator/2_final/app/controllers/home_controller.rb
class HomeController < ApplicationController
  def index
    render inline:
      "<%= link_to 'Translate from English to Polish', '/translator/en/pl' %>"
  end
end
```

With the setup done, we're ready to create our first Devise model, called Admin:

```
$ rails g devise Admin
```

and then run the migration the generator adds:

```
$ bundle exec rake db:migrate
```

At this point, we haven't made any significant changes to our application, but if we run our integration tests, they will fail. This is because the fixtures generated for the Admin have to be properly filled in. However, since we won't need those fixtures for now, let's delete the fixtures file at test/fixtures/admins.yml to make our tests pass again.

To see how Devise works with our application, feel free to fire up a new server, visit /admins/sign_up, create a new admin account, and sign in. You can also access /admins/edit if you want to change your account (although you may want to disable this sign-up ability before deploying the app).

Devise provides several helpers to restrict access to Rails controllers. Since we created a model called Admin, we can use authenticate_admin!() as a before filter, and the request will proceed only if an admin model is authenticated:

```
class PostsController < ApplicationController
  before_filter :authenticate_admin!
end
```

However, we want to add authentication to our Sinatra app, where Devise doesn't include any helpers. Fortunately, this is still trivial to achieve with Devise because of Warden. Whenever we invoke authenticate_admin!() in a Rails controller, it executes the following:

```
env["warden"].authenticate!(scope: "admin")
```

The env["warden"] object is a proxy Warden middleware created, and Devise adds this middleware to the Rails middleware stack via a Rails::Engine. Since this middleware is executed before the request hits the router, the proxy object is also available in Sinatra, and we can easily add authentication to Translator::App in a before callback:

```
translator/2_final/lib/translator/app.rb
before do
  env["warden"].authenticate!(scope: "admin")
end
```

Overall, our request goes through our application and middleware stack, as the following figure shows.

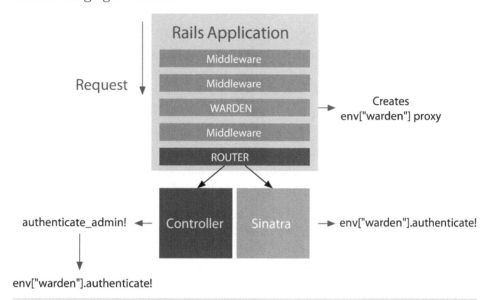

Figure 18—The middleware stack and Rack applications involved in a request to a Rails app with Sinatra, Warden, and Devise

Now when you request the Sinatra application without an admin signed in, the before filter will throw an error. The Warden middleware catches this error using Ruby's *throw/catch*, allowing Warden to redirect you to the sign-in page inside Devise. Once you sign in, the previous code will simply return the current admin in session, proceeding with the Sinatra request.

Although this approach allows us to use the same authentication mechanism across different Rack applications, it has one issue: it requires us to change the Sinatra application by adding a before filter. That said, if we're using a third-party Sinatra application, like the one provided in the Resque gem,[8] we won't be able to modify it.

---

8.   https://github.com/resque/resque

In this case, we could ensure authentication at the router level without needing to change the Sinatra application, as shown here:

```
authenticate "admin" do
  mount Translator::App, at: "/translator"
end
```

Devise adds the previously shown authenticate() to the Rails router, and it simply uses the router's constraint API to ensure the "admin" role is authenticated. Let's check the method implementation in the Devise source code:

```
def authenticate(scope)
  constraint = lambda do |request|
    request.env["warden"].authenticate!(:scope => scope)
  end
  constraints(constraint) do
    yield
  end
end
```

Regardless of whether we choose a before filter or a router constraint to require authentication in our Sinatra application, we can check if the translator back end is now secure by rerunning our test suite and watching it fail.

```
1) Error:
test_can_translate_messages_from_a_given_locale_to_another(TranslatorAppTest)
  Capybara::ElementNotFound: Unable to find field "date.formats.default"
```

The test cannot find the "date.formats.default" label given to fill_in() because it is showing the /admin/sign_in page instead of the translations page. To fix it, let's authenticate an admin in our integration test using a setup hook:

```
translator/2_final/test/integration/translator_app_test.rb
setup { sign_in(admin) }

def admin
  @admin ||= Admin.create!(
    email: "admin_#{Admin.count}@example.org",
    password: "12345678"
  )
end

def sign_in(admin)
  visit "/admins/sign_in"
  fill_in "Email",    with: admin.email
  fill_in "Password", with: admin.password
  click_button "Sign in"
end
```

With this code in place, let's run our test suite again and watch it pass! Notice we decided to manually sign in the admin by filling out the form instead of using a hack that modifies the session or passes in a cookie. In fact, even if we wanted to modify the session or a cookie, Capybara would not allow us to do that—for good reason, as we'll see next.

Adding Cross-Browser Testing

Every time we've used Capybara throughout the book, we've created our own test case called ActiveSupport::IntegrationCase instead of using ActionController::IntegrationTest:

```
# Define a bare test case to use with Capybara
class ActiveSupport::IntegrationCase < ActiveSupport::TestCase
  include Capybara
  include Rails.application.routes.url_helpers
end
```

While writing Rails integration tests using ActionController::IntegrationTest, we have full access to the raw request and response objects, allowing us to check and manipulate cookies, sessions, headers, and so on. Capybara, on the other hand, has a very closed API that does not expose these. That said, if we simply included Capybara in ActionController::IntegrationTest, we would be tempted to access and manipulate these objects, leading to both conceptual and practical issues.

Let's discuss the conceptual issues a bit. Capybara was designed to let us write integration tests from the mindset of an end user. For example, imagine we're building an ecommerce site that keeps in the footer the last five products we viewed. If our implementation is simply storing these product IDs in the session, a naive integration test would simply assert that, after accessing a product page, the product ID was added to the session.

The issue with this kind of test is that the ecommerce user does not care if something was stored in the session. The user just wants to see the last-visited products in the footer and be able to click them, something we did not assert in our tests.

Besides, the fact that we store this information in the session is an implementation detail. If at some point we decide to keep this data in a cookie, our naive test will fail, but it should pass since the user interface has not changed at all. This is a common symptom in tests too coupled to their implementation.

For this reason, Capybara hides all these internals from you, which works out well considering that one of Capybara's most important features is that it supports different drivers. Capybara drivers manipulate a browser, which then accesses our application through a web server, as the following figure shows.

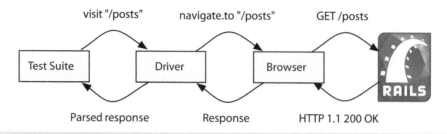

Figure 19—Call trace when using Capybara with a Selenium driver and Firefox

Some drivers, such as Selenium, use common browsers (Firefox, Internet Explorer, and Chrome), while others interact with a headless browser like PhantomJS.

As you may expect, each browser Selenium supports must expose a limited API. Some may expose access to cookies; others may not. Some headless browsers may give you full control of request headers, but others do not. To allow you to switch drivers and browsers without a need to rewrite a huge part of your integration tests, Capybara focuses on the common set that most of them support.

By default, Capybara uses the Rack test driver, which bypasses the whole browser and accesses the Rack application directly. This is very convenient in terms of performance, but it's also very limited. For example, any feature that relies on JavaScript can't be tested with the default driver. Luckily, we can easily change our applications to use another driver. Let's give Selenium a try in our application by adding the following lines to our test helper:[9]

translator/2_final/test/test_helper.rb
```
require "selenium-webdriver"

# Can be :chrome, :firefox or :ie
Selenium::WebDriver.for :firefox
Capybara.default_driver = :selenium

class ActiveSupport::TestCase
  # Disable transactional fixtures for integration testing
  self.use_transactional_fixtures = false
end
```

---

9.   http://seleniumhq.org/

Selenium uses real browsers to test our application. By default it uses Firefox,[10] which you need to have installed before running tests again. After you install it, run our integration tests, and notice that Selenium is automatically starting Firefox and driving it against our website! At the end, our tests still pass!

Because Selenium needs to access a web server for each request, Capybara automatically starts one up. Since Capybara fires this new web server in a thread, the database connection used in tests is not the same one the server uses in each request. That said, if we use transactional fixtures to wrap each test in a database transaction, the data created in tests won't be available in the server since transactional data is not shared between database connections until it is committed. This is why we need to disable transactional fixtures in our test/test_helper.rb file, even though it reduces performance.

Another consequence of disabling transactional fixtures is that the data stored in our database is not cleaned up between tests, and this will definitely get in the way as we add new tests to our suite. Fortunately, a few solutions do all this work for us. One that stands out is Database Cleaner,[11] since it supports different object-relational mappers and databases.

8.5 Wrapping Up

In this chapter, we created another Rails application and used the opportunity to better describe how Rails applications are structured and designed. We've once again seen the importance of the Rack specification and how it makes it easy for different frameworks (such as Rails and Sinatra) to play along with each other without hassle. We also talked more about I18n, its back ends, and its extensions. Plus, we found a good case for using a simple key-value store as Redis.

Finally, we discussed two gems that are widely used in the Rails community: Devise and Capybara. I advise you to take the next step and play with them a bit more—not only using them, but checking out their source code. You'll notice how Devise uses ActionController::Metal, as we saw in *Playing with Metal*, on page 57, to define a bare-bones controller, and you'll learn how Capybara uses Rack applications and handlers to automatically start up servers.

That concludes our tour of Rails. The tools we discussed (the rendering stack, railties, engines, generators, Active Model, and so on) are powerful not only

---

10. http://www.mozilla.com/firefox/
11. https://github.com/bmabey/database_cleaner

for the development of Rails extensions and applications, but also for the development of Rails itself.

While developing your next web application or maintaining an existing one, remember all the tools available to make your code cleaner. You can use responders to DRY up your controller and use generators to keep you and your team productive. Now you can analyze other Rails extension source code, submit changes, and debug problems with greater ease.

Finally, you understand Rails better. You can explore other areas of the source code; study other Action Controller and Active Model modules; check other generator implementations; or read the source of railties, engines, and applications in detail! Rails also has detailed guides on how to contribute to Rails,[12] so if you haven't done so yet, this is the time to propose improvements or fix some bugs that may have been bothering you.

I hope this book has taught you new ways to improve your Ruby code and Rails applications. Most of all, I hope you had fun.

—José Valim

---

12. http://guides.rubyonrails.org/contributing_to_rails.html

Index

Put the "Fun" in Functional

Elixir puts the "fun" back into functional programming, on top of the robust, battle-tested, industrial-strength environment of Erlang.

You want to explore functional programming, but are put off by the academic feel (tell me about monads just one more time). You know you need concurrent applications, but also know these are almost impossible to get right. Meet Elixir, a functional, concurrent language built on the rock-solid Erlang VM. Elixir's pragmatic syntax and built-in support for metaprogramming will make you productive and keep you interested for the long haul. This book is *the* introduction to Elixir for experienced programmers.

Dave Thomas
(240 pages) ISBN: 9781937785581. $36
http://pragprog.com/book/elixir

A multi-user game, web site, cloud application, or networked database can have thousands of users all interacting at the same time. You need a powerful, industrial-strength tool to handle the really hard problems inherent in parallel, concurrent environments. You need Erlang. In this second edition of the best-selling *Programming Erlang*, you'll learn how to write parallel programs that scale effortlessly on multicore systems.

Joe Armstrong
(548 pages) ISBN: 9781937785536. $42
http://pragprog.com/book/jaerlang2

The Joy of Math and Healthy Programming

Rediscover the joy and fascinating weirdness of pure mathematics, and learn how to take a healthier approach to programming.

Mathematics is beautiful—and it can be fun and exciting as well as practical. *Good Math* is your guide to some of the most intriguing topics from two thousand years of mathematics: from Egyptian fractions to Turing machines; from the real meaning of numbers to proof trees, group symmetry, and mechanical computation. If you've ever wondered what lay beyond the proofs you struggled to complete in high school geometry, or what limits the capabilities of the computer on your desk, this is the book for you.

Mark C. Chu-Carroll
(282 pages) ISBN: 9781937785338. $34
http://pragprog.com/book/mcmath

To keep doing what you love, you need to maintain your own systems, not just the ones you write code for. Regular exercise and proper nutrition help you learn, remember, concentrate, and be creative—skills critical to doing your job well. Learn how to change your work habits, master exercises that make working at a computer more comfortable, and develop a plan to keep fit, healthy, and sharp for years to come.

This book is intended only as an informative guide for those wishing to know more about health issues. In no way is this book intended to replace, countermand, or conflict with the advice given to you by your own healthcare provider including Physician, Nurse Practitioner, Physician Assistant, Registered Dietician, and other licensed professionals.

Joe Kutner
(254 pages) ISBN: 9781937785314. $36
http://pragprog.com/book/jkthp

The Modern Web

Get up to speed on the latest HTML, CSS, and JavaScript techniques.

HTML5 and CSS3 are more than just buzzwords—they're the foundation for today's web applications. This book gets you up to speed on the HTML5 elements and CSS3 features you can use right now in your current projects, with backwards compatible solutions that ensure that you don't leave users of older browsers behind. This new edition covers even more new features, including CSS animations, IndexedDB, and client-side validations.

Brian P. Hogan
(300 pages) ISBN: 9781937785598. $38
http://pragprog.com/book/bhh52e

With the advent of HTML5, front-end MVC, and Node.js, JavaScript is ubiquitous—and still messy. This book will give you a solid foundation for managing async tasks without losing your sanity in a tangle of callbacks. It's a fast-paced guide to the most essential techniques for dealing with async behavior, including PubSub, evented models, and Promises. With these tricks up your sleeve, you'll be better prepared to manage the complexity of large web apps and deliver responsive code.

Trevor Burnham
(104 pages) ISBN: 9781937785277. $17
http://pragprog.com/book/tbajs

Explore Testing and Cucumber

Explore the uncharted waters of exploratory testing and delve deeper into Cucumber.

Uncover surprises, risks, and potentially serious bugs with exploratory testing. Rather than designing all tests in advance, explorers design and execute small, rapid experiments, using what they learned from the last little experiment to inform the next. Learn essential skills of a master explorer, including how to analyze software to discover key points of vulnerability, how to design experiments on the fly, how to hone your observation skills, and how to focus your efforts.

Elisabeth Hendrickson
(160 pages) ISBN: 9781937785024. $29
http://pragprog.com/book/ehxta

Your customers want rock-solid, bug-free software that does exactly what they expect it to do. Yet they can't always articulate their ideas clearly enough for you to turn them into code. *The Cucumber Book* dives straight into the core of the problem: communication between people. Cucumber saves the day; it's a testing, communication, and requirements tool – all rolled into one.

Matt Wynne and Aslak Hellesøy
(336 pages) ISBN: 9781934356807. $30
http://pragprog.com/book/hwcuc

The Pragmatic Bookshelf

The Pragmatic Bookshelf features books written by developers for developers. The titles continue the well-known Pragmatic Programmer style and continue to garner awards and rave reviews. As development gets more and more difficult, the Pragmatic Programmers will be there with more titles and products to help you stay on top of your game.

Visit Us Online

This Book's Home Page
http://pragprog.com/book/jvrails2
Source code from this book, errata, and other resources. Come give us feedback, too!

Register for Updates
http://pragprog.com/updates
Be notified when updates and new books become available.

Join the Community
http://pragprog.com/community
Read our weblogs, join our online discussions, participate in our mailing list, interact with our wiki, and benefit from the experience of other Pragmatic Programmers.

New and Noteworthy
http://pragprog.com/news
Check out the latest pragmatic developments, new titles and other offerings.

Save on the eBook

Save on the eBook versions of this title. Owning the paper version of this book entitles you to purchase the electronic versions at a terrific discount.

PDFs are great for carrying around on your laptop—they are hyperlinked, have color, and are fully searchable. Most titles are also available for the iPhone and iPod touch, Amazon Kindle, and other popular e-book readers.

Buy now at *http://pragprog.com/coupon*

Contact Us

Online Orders:	*http://pragprog.com/catalog*
Customer Service:	*support@pragprog.com*
International Rights:	*translations@pragprog.com*
Academic Use:	*academic@pragprog.com*
Write for Us:	*http://pragprog.com/write-for-us*
Or Call:	+1 800-699-7764

CPSIA information can be obtained at www.ICGtesting.com
Printed in the USA
LVOW01s2354131113

361168LV00011B/22/P